Presented by the
Women's Missions & Ministries
Department

LIVE THE CALL

Embrace God's Design for Your Life

Wanda Lee

new
hope
PUBLISHERS

Birmingham, Alabama

New Hope® Publishers
P. O. Box 12065
Birmingham, AL 35202-2065
www.newhopepublishers.com

Library of Congress Cataloging-in-Publication Data

Lee, Wanda, 1949-
  Live the call : embrace God's design for your life / Wanda Lee.
      p. cm.
  ISBN 1-56309-994-2 (softcover)
  1. Vocation--Christianity. 2. Missions. I. Title.
  BV4740.L44 2006
  266--dc22
                                        2006001319

All Scripture quotations, unless otherwise indicated, are taken from the HOLY BIBLE, NEW INTERNATIONAL VERSION®. NIV®. Copyright ©1973, 1978, 1984 by International Bible Society. Used by permission of Zondervan. All rights reserved.
   Scripture quotations marked KJV are taken from The Holy Bible, King James Version.
   Scripture quotations marked NKJV are taken from the New King James Version. Copyright© 1982 by Thomas Nelson, Inc. Used by permission. All rights reserved.
   Scripture quotations marked CEV are taken from the Contemporary English Version. Copyright © 1995 American Bible Society.
   Scripture quotations marked The Message are taken from The Message by Eugene H. Peterson. Copyright © 1993, 1994, 1995, 1996, 2000, 2001, 2002. Used by permission of NavPress Publishing Group.

ISBN-10: 1-56309-994-2
ISBN-13: 978-1-56309-994-6
N064127•0506•8M1

CONTENTS

ACKNOWLEDGEMENTS

Writing a book, especially your first book, is a daunting task. Anyone who has ever tried can attest to the fact that writing requires discipline, patience, and determination. I'm grateful for the training received across the years from some of the best at WMU, professionals who willingly shared their knowledge, skills, and gently guided my early attempts at putting words on paper.

I'm grateful for a WMU tradition of collaboration where the talents of both laypeople and professionals are utilized in designing emphases, curriculum, books, and more. This book is the result of one of those collaborative processes where staff, state leaders, and volunteers developed the emphasis Live the Call. With much encouragement from WMU staff, I accepted the challenge of trying to communicate basic principles that can help us understand, embrace, and live God's call.

It has also been a privilege to share life experiences with many whose stories are found within these pages. Their willingness to trust me to communicate their understanding of God's call has been a special privilege. Most of all, I'm grateful for a supportive family that provided encouragement and support while sacrificing family time in this process. They have been my greatest teachers and cheerleaders in this project and in life as I have sought to live the call God placed on my life so long ago.

INTRODUCTION

My personal story

Today is my anniversary. There will not be any fanfare. No special dinner out or gifts to mark the occasion—only a few moments of reflection while sitting quietly in my favorite chair in the den of my home. Before you think my husband is one of those who can't remember special dates, let me assure you he has never once forgotten our anniversary, my birthday, or any other significant event in our 34 years of marriage. He even surprised me with a beautiful ring one year on a cold day in January at a romantic restaurant. It wasn't a special occasion as far as I could remember, but it was to him. Twenty-five years earlier on that date he had proposed marriage, marking the beginning of our journey together as life partners.

No, today is not my wedding anniversary. Today is a private anniversary that probably no one else will remember or think important but me. Today marks the day I took a significant step in my personal journey of understanding and following God's call in my life.

Five years ago today, I woke up in a strange apartment in a new city far away from my husband and the life I had known for nearly 20 years. I got up early, read my Bible quietly on the screened-in porch, ate breakfast, dressed in a navy blue suit, and then drove across the highway to begin the first day of a new and very different life. It was the day I began serving as the executive director of what has been referred to as the largest organization of laypeople in the world—Woman's Missionary Union® (WMU®). WMU is a religious, nonprofit organization located in Birmingham, Alabama. Our building sits on top of New Hope Mountain, overlooking the fastest growing area of the city. It is a publishing company, a consulting firm, and a church services organization for the Baptist denomination. It is the home to Baptist Nursing Fellowship℠, a creative international ministries network, and more. WMU is many things, and yet it has remained focused on one overriding purpose since its inception—to equip people with an understanding of the mission of God and to help them find ways to be personally involved in fulfilling that mission.

On that first morning five years ago many thoughts raced through my mind, but the most prominent ones were: *How on earth did I get to this place in my life? What was I thinking when I said yes to the committee who invited me to accept this overwhelming job?* Those questions have surfaced numerous times in my mind throughout the past five years, but when I reflect on how God has led me in the past, I can see His hand in this as well.

There have been four times in my life when I have clearly heard God's call. The first was a call to faith at the age of eight. It wasn't a dramatic conversion since I had always gone to church, but it was a time when I knew I needed to make a decision—follow God's call by inviting Jesus to become my personal Savior or say no. I'm so glad I said yes and can say without hesitation it was the greatest decision I have ever made.

My second clear and compelling call came following my senior year in high school when I knew beyond a shadow of doubt God was calling me to serve Him vocationally as a nurse. For more than 30 years, I practiced that profession with joy, knowing it was a part of His plan for my life.

A third call from God came over a period of time where much soul-searching and the counsel of others helped clarify what I was hearing. It was a call to career service as a missionary. God, through a series of events and people, revealed His call to both my husband and me. It was a significant, life-changing experience for both of us.

And now the fourth call, just as clear and distinct as the others and, yes, just as life-altering. This call was the culmination of a lifelong journey of seeking to understand, embrace, and live the call of God in my life. It was the opportunity to lead the organization that had greatly influenced my life choices and challenged me to give all that I am back to God for His service. This call seemed more difficult than all the others. This call required leaving the home where we raised our children, leaving the hospital where I had served for 18 years. But more than that, it meant my husband would have to give up his avenue of service. It was not a decision that came easily or quickly, but God's call continued in the midst of the struggle.

My response to God's call was far from pretty to say the least. For more than a year, I fought it by telling the committee that I wasn't interested each time they asked, "Are you sure God is not calling you to this task?" It seems He told them while He was trying to get through to me. After all, I had many good, legitimate reasons for why I didn't even want to consider that God might be calling me to this role, so I refused to even think about it. First of all, my husband was completing his tenth year as the director of pastoral care for a hospital system; a job he loved and had developed from nothing. I would never ask him to give that up for me to take a job in another state. Secondly, my life was good. Our children were in college; our home was paid for; we were involved in a church where we were encouraged to exercise our gifts; and I loved my work as a nurse. One of my great joys for more than 25 years had been to work with teenage girls through Acteens®, a missions organization in the church that helps girls discover God's call for their lives. We were having a wonderful year seeing these girls mature, learn how to serve others, and discover that God has a great plan for their lives. Why would I give that up for the stress of denominational life, the challenges of supervising more than 125 staff members, and a job so far outside of my training as a nurse? It was insane to even think about it; so I didn't. When the committee called for the third time, my husband had the nerve to ask if I had prayed about this job. I told him no and that I didn't intend to. In his very wise and caring way, he simply looked at me and said, "If God is calling you to this task and you say no because of me, we are both going to be in trouble. If He is calling you, He also has something in store for me."

And so, I come back to the question I started with, "How

on earth did I get to this place in my life? If life as I knew it was so good, so stable, so meaningful, why did I leave it behind?" It's really quite simple. I knew the moment I asked God to make His will known to me He would do just that. God's call to this place at this time in my life was as clear as anything I had ever experienced. The process with the committee and then with the board of directors for WMU, as they issued the invitation to move into this leadership role, confirmed God's call as well. His presence immediately became an overwhelming source of affirmation and strength in my life. All that He previously led me to do in my life seemingly came together for this task. I have learned that no experience is wasted when we recognize that God is in control. The skills gained from my work as a nurse, my life as a missionary, pastor's wife, and mother would provide the basis for all that was ahead.

Leading the largest organization of laypeople engaged in missions is a privilege I do not take for granted. If I have found any success, I think it is because I am simply a woman of the church, a laywoman who continues with the task of developing as a follower of Christ. I believe that God calls each one of us to faith and then to a life of service. He gives each of us unique gifts that only we can contribute to the overall life of His body, the church. My journey has been one of discovering God's call all along the path where He has led. I wish I could say I have always been faithful to every aspect of His call. I have not, and I am certain I have missed some great blessings along the way. But when I have followed His call, I have found the experience to be a testimony of God's power at work in and through me despite all my imperfections. I have discovered that when we commit all that we are and all the resources we have to His purposes, He can accomplish incredible things through our lives.

At the age of 14, Mattie Stepanek was a recognized poet and philosopher. His body devastated by a serious neuromuscular disorder since birth, he spent much of his time confined to a wheelchair, connected to oxygen, and on a respirator. I watched an interview on *Good Morning America* one day as one of Mattie's dreams came true—to meet former President Jimmy Carter. Mattie was speechless for a moment and then, as if they were two adult friends, they began to talk about why they wrote. Mattie wanted to be sure his message about living life to the fullest and his desire to be a peacemaker was heard. He wanted to be sure that when others looked at his challenges in life, they were accompanied with words of hope and encouragement for others to live fully regardless of life's circumstances. He believed he had been created for a purpose and wanted to live his life to the fullest, whatever that meant.

Reportedly, shortly before his death Mattie asked his mother, "Have I done enough? Will the message live on?" Indeed he had done enough, and in his short life, he came to realize he had a tremendous influence on others, and therefore all he had endured was worth it. He had lived the call God had placed on his life with all the gusto and enthusiasm he could find.

To live the call God places on each of our lives requires that we recognize that God is always calling us first to

Himself. When we submit all that we are, all that we have and hope to be to Him, His presence becomes such a driving force that we can do no less than live fully devoted to following His call wherever it may lead. My prayer for each of us is that we will make the effort to begin and continue the journey of discovering God's call, that we will embrace God's design for our lives in such a way that we will know living His call really is worth it!

Wanda S. Lee

March 1, 2005

SECTION 1

UNDERSTAND THE MISSION OF GOD

We've a story to tell to the nations,
That shall turn their hearts to the right,
A story of truth and mercy,
A story of peace and light,
A story of peace and light.

We've a song to be sung to the nations,
That shall lift their hearts to the Lord,
A song that shall conquer evil,
And shatter the spear and sword,
And shatter the spear and sword.

We've a message to give to the nations,
That the Lord who reigneth above
Hath sent us His Son to save us,
And show us that God is love,
And show us that God is love.

We've a Savior to show to the nations,
Who the path of sorrow hath trod,
That all of the world's great peoples
May come to the truth of God,
May come to the truth of God.

For the darkness shall turn to dawning,
And the dawning to noonday bright,
And Christ's great kingdom shall come on earth,
The kingdom of love and light.

The Baptist Hymnal (1991 edition)

The hymn writer penned these words long ago as an expression of his understanding of God's call to every believer. When we come to faith we discover a God who loves us and changes our lives. He gives our lives purpose and a message worth telling to all who will listen.

Purpose in life fuels passion for the things we spend our time doing. As believers we become driven by a passion to know and understand God's specific will for our lives. Knowing and understanding the mission of God provides focus and direction. It helps us see the roadblocks preventing us from becoming all God is calling us to be. It also becomes the stabilizing force when everything else around us may be in chaos.

To live the call of God in our lives means we know the One who calls us; we understand who He is and what His mission is in the world. How can we know Him and understand His mission? It begins as we develop a close relationship with Him through His Son, Jesus Christ. It continues with our understanding of His Word and how we are to imitate His lifestyle. Through the presence and power of the Holy Spirit we are able to understand the mission of God in today's world and allow His view of the world become ours.

CHAPTER 1

WHAT'S WORTH IT?

"As long as I see any thing to be done for God, life is worth
having; but O how vain and unworthy it is to live for any
lower end!"

David Brainerd[1]

A rather anxious-looking petite woman pushed her way
through the crowd of several hundred people gathered at the
school. Word had spread throughout this small town in
northwest Brazil that a team of American medical personnel
were offering free medical care on a first-come, first-served
basis. She came hoping to see a doctor, not for herself, but to
ask for help for her 20-year-old daughter. I was working

triage for the three doctors, a new experience in itself but one made even more challenging since I could not speak the language. I was so grateful for an interpreter who did her best to help me gain basic information as I assessed each person's situation. That's when I saw the petite woman pushing her way towards me. Without hesitation, her story unraveled through rapid and sometimes emotional expressions. Her daughter had given birth sometime in the past week; the baby died; her husband left her; and now she was very sick, too sick to wait in the long line that now numbered over 500 people. I could see by the panic in the woman's eyes that she was desperate for help. I sent her home with instructions to bring her daughter to a room near my workstation and to let me know when they were there.

It wasn't long before both mother and daughter appeared. With one look I knew she was indeed very ill. Her skin was flushed and hot to the touch, eyes weak and yellowing. She could barely stand with assistance, let alone by herself. One of the doctors, having previously committed to live and work in this country, was fluent in Portuguese and began to assess her condition immediately. He shared how so often women in this part of Brazil developed infections of various kinds during childbirth, especially if they had to be put to sleep for complications in delivery. This young woman had developed pneumonia in addition to a post-delivery infection. After much conversation among the three of them, none of which I understood, he handed antibiotics and an intravenous set up to me. With a hint of a smile, he challenged me not to miss on my first attempt at inserting the needle since it was his last.

Thanks a lot, I thought to myself. *You could have gone all day without telling me that!* My mind was racing with all kinds of thoughts. First, *What was he thinking? He's got to be kidding.* Then a moment of personal inadequacy: *I can't possibly do this here with only a table for a bed in a dirty schoolroom. There's not an IV pump to regulate the flow of medicine. Why, there's not even an IV pole to hang the bag of fluids on should I be so lucky as to get it started in the first place! Where's all the high-tech equipment when you really need it, and what would the hospital infection control people think if they knew what I was about to do? And what if . . .* Then a moment of reality hit me. I was confronted with a very sick young woman who had been through great trauma already. She wasn't physically able to go somewhere else, and even if she could, neither she nor her mother had the money nor the transportation to do so. This was not about me or my insecurities. I learned from the best teachers that medicine was all about the patient; about using your own five senses to assess, evaluate, and deliver the best care possible under any given circumstances, and to never do any harm. I didn't need high-tech equipment to deliver loving, quality care. I paused, took a deep breath, and began to arrange the room to do the best I could for her. The windows had shutters that opened inward and served well as an IV pole for the medicine. Someone found a pillow and a blanket and transformed the table into a rather firm bed. With the help of my interpreter, I looked at this young woman's face and smiled, gently touched her arm, and told her what I was about to do. She nodded with understanding and voiced a weak thank-you. Once everything was ready, I held the IV needle in my hand, acknowledged my own inadequacy and fear to God, and asked Him to be present in this place as we sought to touch the life of this beautiful young woman.

There have been other times in my life when I knew God was present—times when He intervened and accomplished something that would not have happened if left to me. This was another one of those experiences. The IV went in easily; the fluids and medicine flowed without difficulty; and she began to rest quietly. Throughout the day I stayed close to the room and kept a watchful eye over the medicine, my patient, and her mother. I so wanted to talk with her and reassure her; to comfort her over the loss of her baby, give her a word of encouragement about her husband. All I could do was touch her tenderly, smile, and pray. Frequently I observed my interpreter in quiet conversation with the mother. At one point I saw the mother begin to weep softly and then she smiled. The anxious strain left her face. Then I watched as she laid her head next to her daughter's on the pillow and spoke softly to her. Some time later I noticed tears streaming down her daughter's face as well. Feeling somewhat concerned about what was happening, I went to the interpreter for help.

My interpreter, knowing the language and being sensitive to the needs of this family, had shared her personal story of hope, faith, forgiveness, and healing with a mother who in turn shared this truth with her daughter. Both had professed a new found faith in God as they invited Jesus Christ to become a part of their everyday lives. They left us 12 hours later on the road to healing and wholeness, both physically and spiritually.

That's when I knew that no matter what else happened on this trip to Brazil, it was all worth it. Two weeks of separation from my husband and children, exhaustion from working long hours in 100°F heat, stomach problems that came as a result of unhealthy food and water, cockroaches that joined me each day in the shower and in my house shoes at night. Suddenly none of that mattered. Everything was crystal clear. I knew why I had come to this remote part of the world. My view of the world was so limited. God wanted to help me see the world and the needs of His people through His eyes. The more I allowed Him to teach me, the more He could work through me to make a difference in the lives of people who needed to know Him and experience His love and grace.

Searching

As I have traveled across the United States and to many different countries, I have discovered that many people in our world today are searching for a way to make sense out of their lives. Some have been battered and bruised by serious struggles in life. They move through each day not knowing where their next meal will come from, where they will sleep, or how they will buy medicine should they or their children become ill. They live their lives wondering if today might be their last, as each day presents itself without any thought of a better tomorrow. If lack of physical necessities isn't enough, they search for love in all the wrong places, often moving from one bad relationship to another. The children suffer from a lack of stability in their lives, moving from one school to another, and with each move, different parental influences in their young lives often leads them to the same vicious cycle of abuse, hunger, homelessness, and despair.

In the midst of their life circumstances many people ask: Is this all there is to life? What is the point? Why am I here, and what will make my life worth living?

On the other hand, many people have all the basic necessities of life—access to healthy food, clean water, shelter, and health care. They have completed a high level of education, have a job, and even have enough resources to enjoy many things considered to be a part of "the good life." They've experienced a relatively high degree of stability in their life, affording them the opportunity to put down roots. They live basically free from the threat of violence and have friends and family who love them. They have a sense of family history, maybe even a legacy, worth living up to. You might say they have it all. But they too want to know: Is this all there is to life? Why am I here, and what will make my life worth living?

A wealthy businessman spoke one day at a conference in England near Oxford University. As he related his motivation for making all the money he had made during his life, he paused, and with tears in his eyes, said: "To be honest, one of my motives for making so much money was simple—to have the money to hire people to do what I don't like doing. But there's one thing I've never been able to hire anyone to do for me: find my own sense of purpose and fulfillment. I'd give anything to discover that."[2]

Leaving a legacy

Much has been written in recent years about the desire of some people not just to live successfully but to live significantly. Deep down we want our lives to count for something, to somehow make a lasting difference in the world, to leave behind a legacy worth following. We want to believe there was a reason for our being born, something much larger than ourselves that will inspire us to stretch for that which is beyond our normal reach. For in doing so we think we can finally know why we are here in the first place.

When my brother and I were growing up, our parents always made certain we had the necessities of life. As Christians, church attendance was also a part of our lives. We came to faith early in life through the influence of a wonderful church in south Florida. Even though our parents had very little in the way of material goods, we never felt poor or realized we were lacking in many material things. Life seemed very normal to my way of thinking until I was around age 12. That's when my mother was diagnosed with a brain tumor, and our ordinary life turned into something quite different. With the help of family and friends, my brother and I managed to stay in school, assume most of the household duties, and treasure the fact that Mom was still with us, even though very limited in physical activity. By the time I was 16, her condition worsened, and she and I moved to the town of her birth in Alabama where her mother and sisters lived, leaving my father and brother in Florida. God was very real through it all to my mother and me. We talked of His love for both of us, how He had made it possible for her to live longer than the surgeons' estimate of only six months. It was the beginning of my understanding that God has a plan for each of our lives, and in the process of understanding His plan, we also must learn to rely on Him in all circumstances of life. That time during her illness prepared me to let her go. She was 44, and I was 17.

That was the first time I remember thinking about my future and asking the questions, Why am I here, and what will make my life worth living? I had not prepared for college, thinking I would continue to care for my mother. Through the influence of a teacher and my pastor, God spoke to me in a very real way. Through a series of miracles, I was admitted at the last possible moment to the Baptist Hospital School of Nursing in Birmingham, Alabama. I soon discovered the second great calling in my life. My first calling had been to a faith relationship with God, and now my second calling was to a life of service as a nurse. The answers to my questions about purpose were beginning to emerge.

I can tell you exactly when I knew God had called me to serve vocationally as a nurse. I already had an overwhelming sense of rightness because of the miracles related to my being accepted at the school in the first place, but that sense of calling came a few weeks later. During what was referred to at that time as Christian Emphasis Week, various speakers came to the school to share their personal stories of following God's call in their lives. One night a young woman who had completed two years serving in the Middle East as a missionary shared stories of her harrowing experiences in the midst of war. It was the mid-1960s, and the violence that continues today in that part of the world was raging even then. While I found her stories fascinating, exciting, and frightening all at the same time, it was not her story that God used to confirm His plan for my life's vocation. It was the words she closed with that evening. She simply said: "You are being given a wonderful gift, the gift of an education that God can use. If you will give that gift back to Him, He will do incredible things with it and with your life."

I tucked her words away in my heart as I worked my way through school. Then one Sunday at church, I made my way to the pastor at the conclusion of worship and said the words out loud, "I want to give my life back to God to use as He wishes, wherever He calls me to serve." God had gifted me with a vocation that He could use as an entry point into the lives of hurting people. His call to the nursing profession was as real as anything I had ever known. I was beginning to see that there was purpose and meaning in life if lived in relationship to God's call. It gave me a sense of confidence and assurance that together with God, I could face whatever came in this life.

Over the next few years I was actively engaged in the profession of nursing. I pursued further training at various junctures in the areas of intensive care, dialysis, and in general education towards a degree. I met and married Larry, a ministerial student, who had also experienced God's call to service. While he served as pastor of our first church, I continued my service as a nurse. When our children were born, my professional nursing took a backseat, but I continued to volunteer my skills, caring for church members and at the

American Red Cross. During those years, I experienced the third time in my life when I clearly heard God's call, this time to career missions as a family. It was another moment of discovering why I was here as a part of God's design.

My husband also sensed God's call to missions and was fully committed to explore the possibilities. We put a fleece before God to determine if His call was real: we explained to the mission board of our denomination that we both felt called and were looking for a place where a nurse and a pastor could serve together while each had their own assignment. If we had moments of doubt that the kind of match we were asking for could be found, they were quickly abandoned when we were notified of a request from the Caribbean, on a small island off the coast of Venezuela. St Vincent needed a church planter/pastor and a nurse to help launch a healthcare program to address the needs of malnourished children. It was a match made in heaven! Once again, that sense of rightness and purpose became a clear call from God to serve in this place.

In St. Vincent we discovered that the experience of living in a different culture, of serving in a place where obtaining life's basic necessities becomes a challenge rather than the norm, is life changing. You gain a perspective on what is important in life, what biblical faith is as compared to an Americanized version of spirituality, what it means to depend on God more and less on your own resources. I will forever be grateful for our experience as career missionaries because it continued the refining process in my spiritual journey of discovering the answer to the question, Why am

I here? It taught me the importance of following God's call, no matter where that call might lead.

It also was a time of learning to deal with uncertainty and adversity. Our youngest child was never really well the entire time we lived on the island. His asthmatic condition worsened in the intense humidity and made his life miserable. During one of the most serious episodes in his young life, we realized that for some unknown reason, our time of service in the Caribbean was over; that as parents, we had an obligation to secure the best medical care possible for him, and we returned home

It was a dark time for me as I tried to sort out what I had truly known as God's call to career mission service as a nurse and my responsibility as a wife and mother. For the first time, following God's call was not always clear nor something I agreed with. It was a struggle, but out of the struggle came a fresh new relationship of dependence on Him that would carry me through other challenges in life.

Begin with Jesus

God's call is not a one-time event that is limited to a location. His call is to a way of life—a life of serving others in whatever place we find ourselves, regardless of the obstacles we may face; a way of moving us closer toward an understanding of what makes life worth it. The beginning point for each person is always at the same place—the first call in life is to a personal relationship with Jesus Christ. It is saying yes to His gift of salvation and grace that comes only from God through Christ's death on the Cross. Once that is settled, once we have acknowledged that there is Someone higher and greater than we are, that God is the Creator of all of life including us, we can begin the journey of discovering what makes life worth living.

The search for meaning, for discovering what makes all of life worthwhile, doesn't take place in a vacuum. It is discovered in the everyday journey of life as we weigh choices and opportunities presented before us. I believe it begins with a deep desire to know God and to understand His will for our lives as well. As the Creator of all of life, God is our Father. He loves us unconditionally and wants only the best for us. That does not mean our lives will be free from pain, suffering, difficulties, or challenges. What it does mean is that no matter what comes in life, He will be there to walk with us through it all.

Within each of us is the possibility of discovering God's design for our lives. In discovering and following His call we will find what makes life worthwhile. But with every journey there is always the potential for roadblocks, many of which may be of our own making.

Roadblocks

One of the common roadblocks voiced by people today as they try to discover what makes life worthwhile, whether it relates to their work, family, or church life, is lack of time. Since the number of hours in a day has not changed, it might be that the management of those hours is lacking. In the book *When It's Rush Hour All Day Long*, author John Tadlock identifies a predator that consumes the energy and vitality for living in more and more people every day. He writes of a condition called "hurry sickness," which he describes as "the continuous struggle to accomplish more and more things, participate in more and more activities or events, in less and less time, often in the face of real or imagined opposition from others. In other words, hurry sickness is loading ourselves to the hilt with the 'stuff' of life."[3]

Hurry sickness can be a roadblock to living a life that matters. When we become so busy that we fail to allow any time for quiet reflection, for moments to think and be aware of God's presence in our lives, we can lose our ability to prioritize and determine what is important in life—what is really worthy of our time and energy.

Think about it for a moment. What is a typical day like in your life? Do you get up early in the morning hoping to get off to a good start for the day? Maybe you're one of the lucky few who begins the day with a few moments of quiet time in prayer and Bible study, a chance to read the paper, enjoy a cup of coffee or tea, take the dog for a walk. If that is the case, be grateful and protect that time. But for many people the morning begins with a mad rush to get dressed while trying to provide breakfast and lunches for the family; hustling kids out the door to catch the bus, carpool, or maybe driving them to school yourself; and then the commute to work begins. The next thing you know, you are fighting the onslaught of rush-hour traffic, thinking about the list of things you must get done, and wondering how on earth that will ever happen. While sitting in traffic you begin to go over your to-do list. You know the times of scheduled appointments, and you begin to wonder which of the unscheduled things you can do in between the scheduled ones. What can you accomplish while waiting on the kids to finish soccer practice or piano lessons? If you take work home with you, could you finish the report that is overdue and catch up on email in one evening? You promised to take a home-cooked meal to the neighbor next door who had surgery. You begin to wish you hadn't promised, but you could just stop at the deli and buy something instead of making a dish. Then it dawns on you that you don't even know what *you* are having for dinner tonight, much less what to do for the neighbor. And then, there's the weekend . . . three different events on Friday night, two games for each child at different ball fields, and a spouse who is out of town for work reasons. At that same moment you wonder if there would be time somewhere in there to see a movie with your friends. By the time the day is over, you have a migraine; the kids are fighting with each other; and you never made it to the neighbor's house with dinner.

Hurry sickness—trying to cram too much into an already overfilled day—has become the priority. When we allow busyness to define what life is worth, it leaves little room for hearing what God is calling us to do much less discovering how to live lives that demonstrate that we know what makes living really worthwhile.

A second roadblock to our ability to prioritize and determine what is important in life is the self-absorbed culture in which we live. There is an overwhelming focus both within and outside the churches in America called "meism." What will make me happy? What is the best thing for me in this situation? Whether pertaining to work, leisure activities, or even the work of the church, many times the first thought to any proposition that comes our way is, *What's in it for me?*

This me-first attitude is reinforced every day by the messages we hear on television and radio. Commercials taunt us with messages of: "Have it your way"; "You deserve a break today"; and buy this more expensive product because "you're worth it." We are inundated with the assurance that we come first before anyone or anything else in life. We are led to believe that whatever we want should come first and come quickly. This meism culture is prevalent among all ages and found in all aspects of our lives, including the church. As a result, many people are seeking their own answers in new places outside the influence of family, church, and Scripture.

In 2003, the Barna Research Group reported that most Americans make important life decisions between the ages of 20 and 29. The report showed that this busy, skeptical generation is making decisions about education, career, and marriage without Christian input. According to the report, only 3 out of 10 Americans in this age range attend church in any given week of the year.

Finding what makes life worth living becomes increasingly difficult when the culture all around us suggests we should think about ourselves first, others last. What God desires for us often never even enters the discussion. When meism reigns, discovering a life worth living is silenced in too many instances.

A third roadblock to finding what makes life worth living is growing cynicism all around us and especially about religion in general. When the headlines of the evening news frequently reveal some scandal among religious leaders in our country, cynicism grows regarding the impact of faith in our daily lives. When Christian leaders are seen on CNN, talk shows, or other religious programming espousing views that are contrary to the teachings of the Bible as we have been taught, or they contradict foundational faith experiences in our lives, we begin to doubt the validity of faith to make a difference.

As we engage personally in the life of a church, we often get to know people really well. Sometimes in those relationships we come face-to-face with hypocrisy that may contribute to an attitude of cynicism. What happens to our faith when we learn that those we worship with on a regular basis, who profess to be followers of Christ, do not actually practice what they profess, that their Monday through Saturday life is far different from what is seen on Sunday? When you hear this person speak strongly in church of the importance of living like Christ every day and then discover this person is known for mistreating his or her employees, a spark of doubt and cynicism can develop. Maybe you learn from neighbors that a husband mistreats his wife verbally or physically or a mother often publicly humiliates her children for their failures. It could be something as subtle as engaging in off-color jokes in the break room at work, cheating on expense reports, or taking company supplies home for private use without permission. The respect we once felt for our neighbor disappears. If the behavior continues over a long period of time and with numerous other people professing a

Sunday religion, the belief that our faith should impact everything we do becomes cloudy. We find ourselves making cynical comments about those who are trying to meld their faith with their daily practice. We question everyone's motivation or personal testimony until one day our own personality is one of a cynical nature.

Many people rationalize this inconsistent behavior by compartmentalizing their lives. In some cases, this is seen in how they reserve faith-based behavior for Sunday and think of the rest of their life as private and separate. They have compartmentalized their lives into separate categories and view their home life, professional life, and personal interests as independent from one another and separate from their spiritual life; in their mind there is no overlap. This type of disjointed thinking creates problems as the church tries to help followers of Christ understand that faith is about all of life, every day, in every situation. When we compartmentalize our lives into this is how I act at work, this is what I do at home, this is how I respond at church, the authenticity of our lives diminishes to the point that we lose all sensitivity to the voice of God. Hypocrisy among professed believers becomes a pathway to cynicism about faith in God. Cynicism can silence the search for how to live a life of worth, a life of significance.

Hurry sickness, a culture of meism, and growing cynicism about organized religion are just three of the potential roadblocks to discovering the answer to the questions, Why am I here, and what will make my life worth living? In his book *The Call*, Os Guinness says, "as modern people, we have too much to live with and too little to live for. Some feel they have time but not enough money; others feel they have money but not enough time. But for most of us, in the midst of material plenty, we have spiritual poverty."[4]

Discovering God's call in our lives provides the missing piece when we are drowning in a sea of busyness, excess, and superficial demands. In his letter to the Colossian Christians, Paul wrote, "Walk worthy of the Lord, fully pleasing Him, being fruitful in every good work and increasing in the knowledge of God" (Colossians. 1:10 NKJV). It is only in discovering God's call, His unique design for our lives, that we can find focus and meaning as we embark on a journey of discovering the answer to the questions, Why am I here, and what will make my life worth living?

Think about:

1. When have you felt inadequate to complete a task?
2. Why did you feel this way?
3. Did God intervene and accomplish something that would not have happened if left to you?
4. How has God influenced your vocational decisions?
5. What roadblocks are currently in your way, holding you back from following God's plan for your life?

CHAPTER 2

LIVING AND ACTIVE WORDS

"Words are the deepest, fullest expression in which God now discloses himself to us, beginning with his calling us. So it is in listening to him, trusting him, and obeying him when he calls that we 'let God be God' in all of his awe and majesty."

Os Guinness, *The Call*[1]

Ann Hasseltine Judson was a woman far ahead of her time. In 1812 she married Adoniram Judson and left the comforts of home to represent the Congregationalist Church as the first American woman appointed as a missionary. During the four-month voyage to Burma, after studying the Scriptures, Ann and Adoniram became convinced that God intended His followers to practice immersion as the scriptural form of baptism. Because this was not the teaching of the church from which they were appointed, they sent word back to the leaders of their denomination that they planned to become Baptists. It was a costly decision. They continued on to Burma without the emotional or financial support of their home churches.

The power of the printed word cannot be disputed when we read stories such as this one. Words influence the thoughts and behaviors of people. Words educate people on new ideas and new ways of acting. But the printed word of the Bible is more powerful than any other book of words. It has been described in the Book of Hebrews as "living and active. Sharper than any double-edged sword, it penetrates even to dividing soul and spirit, joints and marrow; it judges the thoughts and attitudes of the heart" (Hebrews 4:12).

It stands to reason then, that once Ann and Adoniram understood God's Word on baptism, the power of the words of the Bible changed their thinking and direction. After such a dramatic experience with their understanding of Scripture, Adoniram directed most of the early years of his ministry to translating the Bible into the language of the Burmese people so they could read for themselves the words of a loving and forgiving God.

God's Word

Understanding the mission of God and His call in our lives begins with an understanding and appreciation for God's Word. The Bible is the life-changing story of His love for all that He created. He is constantly seeking us with an invitation to come and follow Him, to offer restoration and a sense of completeness in our lives.

This was certainly the experience of David when he became king. He had experienced God's presence and His power at work in his life. He heard God's call to be king clearly and decisively, and he followed. After receiving God's promises through the words of Nathan, the prophet, David knew God's words would be his guide as he led the children of Israel. David offered this prayer in 2 Samuel 7:28–29: "O Sovereign Lord, you are God! Your words are trustworthy, and you have promised these good things to your servant. Now be pleased to bless the house of your servant, that it may continue forever in your sight; for you, O Sovereign Lord, have spoken, and with your blessing the house of your servant will be blessed forever."

Knowing God's heart comes from knowing His words, which become our guide for living. The psalmist also acknowledged the power of God's words when he wrote Psalm 119:

"How can a young man keep his way pure? By living according to your word" (v .9).

"I have hidden your word in my heart that I might not sin against you" (v. 11).

"Your word is a lamp to my feet and a light for my path" (v. 105).

"The unfolding of your words gives light; it gives understanding to the simple" (v. 130).

As believers on the other side of the Cross, we have the added benefit of reading and knowing the words of Christ. It is within our fellowship with Christ that our knowledge of God's words increases, and we are led to a greater understanding of the mission of God in our world. Once we understand His mission we are better able to discern who we are, why we are here, and what He wants us to do. His call in our lives emerges as a clear direction that helps us claim our place within His plans.

Jesus' mission statement

Jesus spent a great deal of time during His earthly ministry teaching, healing, meeting needs, and preparing the disciples for leadership. He used the power of words to catch the attention of those who were around Him, whether He was quoting Scripture or telling stories. He used everyday situations to help people understand His teachings by contrasting things like sheep and goats, trees and fruit, planting and harvesting. In His Sermon on the Mount, He painted a picture of those who would find joy in following Him.

> "Blessed are the poor in spirit, for theirs is the
> kingdom of heaven.
> Blessed are those who mourn, for they will be
> comforted.

Blessed are the meek, for they will inherit the earth.

Blessed are those who hunger and thirst for righteousness, for they will be filled.

Blessed are the merciful, for they will be shown mercy.

Blessed are the pure in heart, for they will see God.

Blessed are the peacemakers, for they will be called sons of God.

Blessed are those who are persecuted because of righteousness, for theirs is the kingdom of heaven.

Blessed are you when people insult you, persecute you and falsely say all kinds of evil against you because of me.

Rejoice and be glad, because great is your reward in heaven, for in the same way they persecuted the prophets who were before you."

Matthew 5:1–12

As followers of Christ today, His words are a powerful force in our lives. We read them over and over, discovering something new and fresh every time. As disciples of Jesus, we can find meaning and direction for what will make our lives worth living through His words.

Several passages in the New Testament have always

stood out to me as critical verses for understanding God's call. First, I am always struck by Jesus' clear understanding of His own calling. In Luke 4 we find Jesus providing an explanation of why He came into the world. He chose verses from Isaiah 61: "The Spirit of the Lord is on me, because he has anointed me to preach good news to the poor. He has sent me to proclaim freedom for the prisoners and recovery of sight for the blind, to release the oppressed, to proclaim the year of the Lord's favor" (Luke 4:18–19).

Jesus knew why He came and wanted others to begin to see also. He knew God's spirit was directing Him into an even greater purpose, as was evidenced later on when He predicted His death, burial, and resurrection as the way of salvation for all people. He wants us to know why we are here, as well, in light of the purpose and mission of God. By claiming God's words from Isaiah as His own, He demonstrated the importance of our understanding of Scripture and applying these words to our everyday lives.

The Great Commandment

Another significant passage is Matthew 22:37–40. One day during an exchange with the Pharisees, Jesus quoted a portion of Deuteronomy 6. He was asked the question, "Which is the greatest commandment in the Law?" He responded by saying, "'Love the Lord your God with all your heart and with all your soul and with all your mind.' This is the first and greatest commandment." But then he added something more: "And the second is like it: 'Love your neighbor as yourself.' All the Law and the Prophets hang on these two commandments."

The significance of Jesus' response to the Pharisees lies in the background of when this command was first spoken in the Old Testament. From Exodus to Deuteronomy, we read about the life of Moses. From the miracle of his being saved as an infant to his breaking away from the life he knew to save his people, we see Moses as a man seeking to follow God's call. It was not always easy for Moses. Some of the things he understood God calling him to were hard. Like many of us, he offered excuses for why he couldn't obey God's call. From doubting his ability to lead, to not being eloquent of speech, to fear of the enemies he might face, we can readily identify with Moses. But God was persistent, and, ultimately, Moses followed. Throughout his life, Moses never gave up trying to discern God's heart for him personally and for the children of Israel. In Deuteronomy 6, after Moses received the Ten Commandments, he went to tell the children of Israel what he had heard from God. It is obvious his desire was to lead them to an understanding of God's heart.

In a nutshell, he laid down for the Israelites the essence of biblical faith with these words: "Hear, O Israel: The Lord our God, the Lord is one. Love the Lord your God with all your heart and with all your soul and with all your strength" (Deuteronomy 6:4–5). For Moses, God's words made the desires of His heart clear; the people were to love Him with everything they had and follow His directions for living their lives. God declared that there was only one God, not many as some believed. And Jehovah God expected His people to love Him with an undivided loyalty. How they lived would demonstrate the depth of their commitment to love Him alone. Only by loving God with their total being would they be able to receive the blessing of the promised land God offered. God's words were a powerful influence on Moses' life.

Jesus knew the story of Moses well, particularly this passage of Scripture from the Old Testament. By repeating the passage, he reiterated for the Pharisees and for us that the first priority in our lives must be to love God holistically with all our heart, soul, mind, and strength. Out of that love will flow a deep love for others and a genuine desire to demonstrate that love in all aspects of our lives.

The Great Commandment summarizes an important teaching in the New Testament. It is repeated by each of three Gospel writers, Matthew, Mark, and Luke, in their own unique writing style. In all three accounts the key word is the same—*love*. Only love can lay the foundation for how we relate to God and to others.

Each writer also listed at least three of the same four words revealing how we are to love God. We are told to love God with all our being; with our heart, soul, mind, and strength. In Jewish thought the word *heart* was felt to be the center for thinking and feeling. The word *soul* refers to our inner self and the depth of love we feel for God. *Mind* refers to our ability to rationalize and *strength* to the intensity within our physical being with which we are to love God. Regardless of the words the Gospel writer chose to describe how we are to love God, the intent was the same. We are to give our whole self to God, all that we are, have, and can become.

Not only is *love* the key word in the Great Commandment, but Jesus declares it is the key to fulfilling all the laws that the Jews held onto as their way of living. Jesus had a deep understanding of the Law, even more so than the rabbis of His day. Jesus knew that the kind of love He was talking about liberated people so they could really know God, not just His laws. It was the kind of love that allowed people to love others who were far different. Jesus wanted those who were listening that day to understand that love unifies how we feel with our response to God, others, and ourselves. When we love God with all our being, that love naturally transfers to those we meet and determines how we view ourselves.

Earlier I referenced our tendency to compartmentalize certain aspects of our lives. One evidence of this can be seen in how we declare our love for God, and yet when something bad happens, say that we hate others. Or we verbalize our love for God and others while consistently making self-deprecating statements. Such actions would seem to indicate while love may be extended to others, we do not love ourselves. Jesus says when we love God with all our heart, soul, mind, and strength, that love will transfer to others and ourselves in healthy ways because it is such a powerful force in our lives.

Understanding this kind of love for God becomes easier when we catch a glimpse of the depth of love He has for each of us. His demonstration of love through Jesus' death on the Cross reminds us that God's love is a sacrificial love, a forgiving love, and an eternal love.

Jesus provided for us many models of loving others. The compassion He felt for those who were ill or suffering came from a heart of love for all people. He talked with His disciples about loving others saying, "My command is this: Love each other as I have loved you. Greater love has no one than this, that he lay down his life for his friends" (John 15:12–13).

One of the most poignant scenes in Scripture is in John 11 when Jesus arrives at the tomb following the death of Lazarus. After Mary falls at His feet saying that Lazarus would not have died if He had been there sooner, Jesus begins to weep. The Jews who were watching said, "See, how he loved him!" (John 11:36). With Mary and Martha among the witnesses, Jesus commands Lazarus to "come out." Many people believed in Jesus as the Son of God after this because of the great power demonstrated in this miracle of healing. It also was a great demonstration of the depth of His love for His friends.

The New Testament is full of instructions on how to love others and the importance of believers demonstrating a God kind of love for others. Paul was a master at communicating God's purposes. He reaffirmed the importance of love God as a foundation for who we are and all we do as Christians. In Romans 12:9–10 he says, "Love must be sincere. Hate what is evil; cling to what is good. Be devoted to one another in brotherly love." And in Romans 13:9–10 he says, "Love your neighbor as yourself. Love does no harm to its neighbor. Therefore love is the fulfillment of the law." In Ephesians 4 He tells us to bear with one another in love and speak the truth in love.

Perhaps the greatest description of loving others is found in the familiar words of 1 Corinthians 13:1–3: "If I speak in the tongues of men and of angels, but have not love, I am only a resounding gong or a clanging cymbal. If I have the gift of prophecy and can fathom all mysteries and all knowledge, and if I have a faith that can move mountains, but have not love, I am nothing. If I give all I possess to the poor and surrender my body to the flames, but have not love, I gain nothing."

As I reflect on my journey of discovering why I am here, and what will make life worth living, I realize I can do nothing unless these principles are the foundation for how I live. When we love God holistically, our priorities begin to be realigned. We place God first, others second, and ourselves last. Loving God with all our heart, soul, mind, and strength will make loving others possible. However, Jesus qualified how we were to love others. His instructions were to love others as we love ourselves. He knew our nature was to be selfish; that all too often we were incapable of loving ourselves. He also knew that if we loved God first, we would be able to love ourselves and others as ourselves, not in our strength but in His.

The Great Commission

As we take on the Great Commandment—loving God above all else and others as ourselves—only then can we reach out to the world and follow the instruction of the Great Commission.

When I have my priorities correctly aligned with God's teaching—when I love Him first with all I am and all I have, and I understand I am to love others as I love myself—whatever roadblocks I may experience to discovering what makes life worth living begin to disappear. I find I am more willing and able to grasp the lifestyle Jesus demonstrated for His disciples and the implications of His lifestyle for my own life. When I read the Great Commission, it suddenly takes on new meaning for me. It becomes another piece of the road map for discovering why I am here and what I am to do with my life.

In Matthew 28:18–20 Jesus said: "All authority in heaven and on earth has been given to me. Therefore go and make disciples of all nations, baptizing them in the name of the Father and of the Son and of the Holy Spirit, and teaching them to obey everything I have commanded you. And surely I am with you always, to the very end of the age." Once and for all, Jesus declared who He was and to whom He belonged. God gave Him the right to perform miracles and to give direction to those who would follow Him. In these final words, He presented the focus of God's love. God didn't reserve His words and His love just for a few chosen people. His desire was that all the nations, all the peoples of the world, might know Him. His plan was for His disciples, those present with Him and those who would come later, to spread His words to all who would listen.

One of the key elements in the Great Commission is Jesus' command to go and make disciples. A disciple is someone who is learning a new way. Jesus had been making disciples of the Twelve for three years. He had taught them the meaning of God's Word, sent them out to perform miracles, and consoled them when they failed. He didn't just teach by words alone; He had modeled for them what it meant to live the Great Commission. Matthew 9:35–38 says: "Jesus went through all the towns and villages, teaching in their synagogues, preaching the good news of the kingdom and healing every disease and sickness. When he saw the crowds, he had compassion on them, because they were harassed and helpless, like sheep without a shepherd. Then he said to his disciples, 'The harvest is plentiful but the workers are few. Ask the Lord of the harvest, therefore, to send out workers into his harvest field.'"

One day, after the larger body of 72 disciples returned from practicing what Jesus taught them, they were filled with joy after seeing many miracles performed. They remarked that even the demons were subject to them. At that moment Jesus reminded them of an important spiritual truth of being a disciple: "Do not rejoice that the spirits submit to you, but rejoice that your names are written in heaven" (Luke 10:20). In essence Jesus was saying not to rejoice in successful service but to remember that joy is found in having a right relationship with Him. Disciples are always learning from the Master Teacher and growing in their relationship with Him as Lord.

The Great Commission reminds us that disciples are to always make more disciples, equipping them to live the Christlike life and to have the knowledge to equip others to become disciples as well. It is to be a cycle: disciples making disciples who will carry on the practice of teaching new disciples what Jesus taught and how He lived.

The words of Jesus are packed with meaning. He always brings clarity and direction as we seek to know God's design for our lives. He spoke the truth when it was not the popular thing to do. He spoke words of love and condemnation, words of chastisement and forgiveness, words of hope in the midst of despair. In the Great Commission, Jesus spoke His last instructions to His followers before ascending to heaven. He had modeled for them what living a life totally committed to God was all about. He demonstrated how they were to minister to all people, from all walks of life, meeting their physical, spiritual, and emotional needs. They witnessed His death and resurrection, and heard His promise of the power that would soon come to equip and enable them to do the work He called them to do—to go and baptize, to teach and make disciples—all in His name.

Jesus knew the disciples well enough to know they would doubt themselves and their ability to do as He instructed. He gave them His promise of the power to do all He commanded if they would remain in Jerusalem and wait. "Do not leave Jerusalem, but wait for the gift my Father promised, which you have heard me speak about. For John baptized with water, but in a few days you will be baptized with the Holy Spirit. . . . But you will receive power when the Holy Spirit comes on you; and you will be my witnesses in Jerusalem, and in all Judea and Samaria, and to the ends of the earth" (Acts 1:4–5,8). Because of their faith and their personal experience with Jesus' words being true, they obeyed. The Book of Acts records the coming of the promised Holy Spirit in all its power. The stories of how God used the disciples and other ordinary people to perform miracles as the early church came into being speaks volumes to us today about the availability of His power to work in our lives as well. It is a reminder that anything God calls us to, any task, any lifestyle, can happen if and when we allow His power to be at work within us.

The Great Commission outlines in a succinct way the expectations for a follower of Christ. It describes the path we are to follow as we grow and develop personally and as we disciple others. But it is also a reminder that His message of grace and salvation was not just for the disciples, nor is it just for us today. It mandates that we share this good news with all the peoples of the world: every tribe, every nation, every people group around the globe. As we ponder the magnitude of this task, we are reminded that the Great Commission is not possible unless it springs from the Great Commandment. It is from the depth of God's love for us that we realize we are first and foremost to love Him with all our heart, soul, mind, and strength. Only this kind of love can compel us to love the whole world enough to go and tell them the good news of Christ. When we allow Scripture to be seen as one complete story of a God who loves all of His creation, enough to send the best He had, His Son, so that all may be reunited with Him in a deep and abiding relationship, we begin to live our lives in a more wholly fashion. We no longer separate our faith, our worship, and our service from our day-to-day living at home and work. We can view life as a gift with a purpose that gives meaning beyond anything the world can provide. Together, these two commands provide the litmus test for our faith. If we truly believe that the power of Christ and God's love for every person can literally transform the worst of lives, we open up ourselves to trusting God with our deepest thoughts and concerns. We allow Him to give direction to our decision making and supply the strength for living each day because we realize the depth of His love for us. With that comes an indescribable joy that will overflow into all aspects of our lives where we cannot help but seize every opportunity to share this wonderful story.

One woman's story

The evening news reported the plight of a woman found alive after surviving several days in her car, which had gone off the road, down an embankment, and become hidden from view in the underbrush. People across the city placed this unnamed woman on prayer lists at churches and businesses. A radiology technician named Janet who worked at the local hospital where the woman was taken heard her story. When she went to visit her, they connected in one of those unusual ways where a deeper level of sharing emerged quickly. They discovered many similarities in their past lives. Janet shared her personal story of coming to faith in God and led the woman to invite Christ into her own life. After a period of time in the hospital, the woman was on the road to recovery in more ways than physical healing. While the story of survival and subsequent conversion of the injured woman is a special story unto itself, the real miracle in this story is found in the woman who had something to share with her, a woman whose life had been miraculously transformed by the power of God at work in her life.

Janet is living proof that God can take the worst of

situations and literally transform a person's life, if He can just get our attention. At age 15, Janet married and had a baby. When her marriage failed, she found herself moving from one bad relationship to another. She became addicted to drugs and alcohol. Her single focus in life became an all-consuming desire for crack cocaine. She lived on the streets doing whatever it took, including prostitution, to find the next hit. Years later, at age 42, homeless and addicted, she found herself pregnant again. She ignored her condition, never sought prenatal care, and did not intend to keep the baby if she did carry it to full term.

With the baby's birth approaching, she collapsed on the street one day. A passerby took her to a hospital emergency room where she received medical care, but more importantly, where she had an encounter with God. In an instant, her journey of discovering what makes life worth living began. Janet wrote in a testimony about her life: "I was filthy, and I felt everyone around me was talking about me. I was so angry with them, but even angrier that I had to leave the crack cocaine behind long enough to deliver. My thoughts were all about getting it over with and back to the streets."

But then something happened while she was waiting for her child to be born. Janet said: "I found God in that moment. I felt He was calling me to a different way of life right there on the delivery table. I had planned to leave the baby with the nurses and to go back to the crack house, but God had a different plan the day that my little girl was born. My craving for drugs left me immediately. For the first time in many years, my thoughts turned to loving myself and my baby."

Following the birth of a healthy, drug-free daughter, also evidence of God's power and grace, Janet began the long process of working her way back to wholeness. A social worker helped her find a place to live and start over. She began to learn how to be a mother. Bible study became a part of her recovery. She began to learn what God expected of those who would follow Him. Before life on the streets, she had worked as a radiology technician and decided to pursue being licensed once again. At some point in her recovery, she connected with Christian Women's Job Corps® (CWJC®), a ministry of WMU®, where she was assigned a mentor. She began to have a sense of hope. Before long, she also discovered unconditional love from God and now the love of her mentor who became her "adopted" family.

That was more than five years ago. Today, Janet is licensed to work in radiology once again. She is a loving mother who speaks often of the gift of help and hope she received from so many. She expresses gratitude for CWJC, her Christian mentor, and what it means to have a second chance. She brings joy to her mentor's life, introduces others to Christ, and models what it means to live a life of worth based on God's call. Janet serves other women today as a mentor herself, giving back by listening and helping women whose lives are in the same condition as hers before she had this life-changing encounter with God. Janet says: "What mattered most to me before I got help was crack cocaine and how to get it. What matters now is my faith, that God can set us free and that there are people who care and want to help us. My hope is my story will give someone hope and courage to change their life."

Life-changing words

Janet knows personally about the power of God . Her testimony affirms that when we love God with all our heart, soul, mind, and strength, when we love others more than we love ourselves, God gives us something of significance for us to do with our lives. He never ceases to call us to live a life worthy of His love and forgiveness. People who have experienced forgiveness this deeply never hesitate to tell others this wonderful news.

The power of God's words and the words spoken by Christ are life-changing. The passages of Scripture referenced in this chapter provide the framework for beginning to discover God's call in our lives. If we wonder what our priorities should be, if we wonder why we have trouble relating to other people or finding some sense of meaning and direction for our lives, understanding God's words, the Great Commandment and the Great Commission in particular, can set us on a path of discovering key truths for our lives. When nothing in this world seems to last very long, Jesus declares His words are everlasting: "Heaven and earth will pass away, but my words will never pass away" (Matthew 24:35). We can trust His words to be a guide for our lives; a pathway to understanding the mission of God directing us into a life that is worthwhile and eternal.

Think about:

1. What are three things we should do to let "God be God"?

2. What did Jesus tell the Pharisees should be our first priority in life?

3. What is meant by the command "love your neighbor as yourself"?

4. Why did Jesus paint word pictures for the people around Him? How did He do this?

5. How can we begin to understand the mission of God and His call in our lives?

CHAPTER 3

DISCIPLES UNDER CONSTRUCTION

Sweetly, Lord, have we heard Thee calling,
"Come, follow Me!"
And we see where Thy footprints falling,
Lead us to Thee.
Footprints of Jesus that make the pathway glow;
We will follow the steps of Jesus where'er they go.

The Baptist Hymnal (1991 edition)

What does it mean to follow in the footsteps of Jesus? We read Scripture and hear God's call to follow and obey His words. We see in the life of Christ the ultimate gift from God, His only Son, who came to make a way for us to have an everlasting relationship with our heavenly Father. Our faith is established and secure, but in everyday living, we find it challenging to follow Jesus. How do we become the person He created us to be and build a life that is worthwhile and meaningful? How do we build a life that allows God to be God, the supreme ruler and guide in our lives?

When we talk about following Jesus, sometimes we say we are disciples of Jesus. Both general and Bible dictionaries contain various definitions of the word *disciple*, but many include the phrase "a follower." In the Christian context, we understand a disciple to be one of the Twelve who followed Jesus and also followers of Jesus today, people who have heard the Lord's invitation to "Come, follow me." Fisher Humphreys, in his book *I Have Called You Friends*, says a disciple is an "apprentice." In the secular world, an apprentice is someone who already knows something about their chosen trade or profession, but they are working alongside a more experienced person to improve their skills. In the Christian sense, Humphreys asserts that we are apprentices of Jesus because, "We are already living our lives as Christians; while we are doing that, we also are learning from rabbi Jesus how to be really good Christians."[1] Disciples today are people who have accepted Jesus as their Lord and Savior and are on the journey of understanding how He wants them to live and what He is calling them to do in the world.

Discipleship, then, is the process of learning that begins when we come to faith and continues throughout our lifetime as we strive to become more like the One we are following, Jesus. When Jesus began His earthly ministry, He demonstrated the importance of discipleship. He issued an invitation to 12 ordinary men with three words; "Come, follow me" (Mark 1:17). When two sets of fishermen brothers, Simon and Andrew, and James and John, heard this invitation, they dropped their nets and followed Jesus. Each time He issued the invitation to what became a group of 12 followers, apprentices so to speak, they dropped what they were doing and followed Him.

But what happened once they followed? Did they immediately know and understand who Jesus was and why He called them? Did they have a clear sense of God's call in their lives? Did they have instant power to perform miracles like Jesus? The four Gospels of Matthew, Mark, Luke, and John reveal it definitely was not an instantaneous change but one that occurred over a period of time as they listened to Jesus' teachings and observed how He related to other people. They were observers of Jesus as He went about meeting the needs of hurting, hungry people everywhere they went. In other words, Jesus discipled the Twelve, and when they reached a certain point in their understanding, they were ready to serve like Jesus. Let's look at some of the ways Jesus discipled them as they learned to become "fishers of men" (Matthew 4:19).

Scripture

Jesus, on occasion, used Scripture to teach the disciples. He grew up attending services in the synagogue and was taught by those who knew the Scriptures. At age 12, we find Him discussing Scriptures with His elders. "They found him in the temple courts, sitting among the teachers, listening to them and asking them questions. Everyone who heard him was amazed at his understanding and his answers" (Luke 2:47).

When His earthly ministry began, following His 40 days in the wilderness, Jesus returned to Galilee. "He taught in their synagogues, and everyone praised him" (Luke 4:15). In Nazareth, when He went to the synagogue, He stood to read the passage from Isaiah 61, referred to in the last chapter as His "mission statement." In this passage, Jesus demonstrated His understanding of why He came and what He was to do (Luke 4:17–21).

Numerous times, the Gospel writers acknowledge Jesus' depth of understanding of Scripture. Jesus used the teachings of the Old Testament to get the writers' attention. Then Jesus expanded their understanding of the Scriptures to make them relevant for how the writers should live. For instance, when Jesus quoted the Great Commandment found in Deuteronomy 6, He added to the passage, "'Love your neighbor as yourself.' All the law and the prophets hang on these two commandments" (Matthew 22:39). Jesus wanted the disciples to understand that following Him meant more than just obeying the law; it was about applying the principles to life and being willing to learn a new way, Christ's way, of serving others.

It was also important to Jesus for the disciples to see that He did not come to do away with the law but to fulfill the prophecies of the Old Testament while demonstrating a new way of life for all people. "Do not think that I have come to abolish the Law or the Prophets; I have not come to abolish them but to fulfill them" (Matthew 5:17). Jesus valued the Scriptures and the foundation they laid for generations before His coming. But He wanted them to understand, in light of the culture and religious teachings of their day, how they were to follow God's purpose for their lives in a new way through a relationship with Him. The foundation for discipleship is studying and applying the teachings of the Bible to the way we live and serve with those we meet.

Prayer

In addition to teaching the disciples Scripture, Jesus modeled for them the importance of prayer. He demonstrated when, where, and how they were to pray. He guided them to an understanding of where their power for service would come from. Jesus challenged them to make prayer a vital part of their lives if they truly desired to follow Him.

Minette Drumwright wrote in her book *The Life That Prays* that prayer is "difficult to describe with mere words. . . . Prayer is not a supernatural credit card. It is not a magic wand to wave away misfortune or a rabbit's foot to keep us from disaster. . . . Real prayer is not a blank check on which God's signature appears, guaranteeing anything on which we set our selfish hearts. . . . Prayer is inviting God into the very midst of our lives." She goes on to quote O. Hallesby who wrote:

"Prayer is something deeper than words. It is present in the soul before it has been formulated in words. And it abides in the soul after the last words of prayer have passed over our lips. Prayer is an attitude of our hearts, an attitude of our mind."[2]

As followers of Jesus we need to be discipled in the area of prayer. There are many passages on prayer in the Bible, but Jesus provides the most extensive training on prayer found in the New Testament. During the Sermon on the Mount, Jesus told His disciples how not to pray (Matthew 6:5–8) and how to pray (Matthew 6:9–13). He talked about the motivation for our praying (Mark 12:40) and the faith required when we pray (Matthew 21:21–22).

What we commonly refer to as the Lord's Prayer came in response to one of the disciples who asked Jesus to teach him how to pray. "Lord, teach us to pray, just as John taught his disciples" (Luke 11:1). What follows has been the model for many followers of Christ to this day as they learned to pray.

"Our Father which art in heaven, hallowed be thy name. Thy kingdom come. Thy will be done, in earth, as it is in heaven. Give us this day our daily bread. And forgive us our debts, as we forgive our debtors. And lead us not into temptation, but deliver us from evil: for thine is the kingdom, and the power, and the glory, forever. Amen" (Matthew 6:9–13 KJV).

Jesus taught the disciples to address God as our Father, to pray in accordance with God's will, that it is OK to ask for daily sustenance, and to acknowledge our need for forgiveness. His prayer demonstrates the importance of being forgiving in our nature as well and asking for God's direction in our lives away from those things that would keep us from following in Christ's footprints.

Jesus' prayer in John 17 reveals in a more in-depth way how we are to pray as we seek to fulfill God's call in our lives. Jesus knew His time was short, so He prayed for Himself, His disciples, and all others who would follow His teachings in the days to come. He clearly established His understanding of His oneness with God.

"Father, the time has come. Glorify your Son, that your Son may glorify you. . . . For I gave them the words you gave me and they accepted them. They knew with certainty that I came from you, and they believed that you sent me. I pray for them. . . . Holy Father, protect them by the power of your name. . . . Sanctify them by the truth; your word is truth. . . . My prayer is not for them alone. I pray also for those who will believe in me through their message, that all of them may be one. . . . May they be brought to complete unity to let the world know that you sent me and have loved them even as you have loved me" (John 17:1, 8–9, 11, 17, 20–21, 23).

As you read Jesus' prayer, you realize it is a very personal time of conversation with the heavenly Father that He loved and sought to serve. His love for the disciples and for those of us who have believed since that day reaffirms the close relationship He had with His Father who demonstrated love supremely on the Cross.

What else can we learn from the Bible about prayer? Jesus said we "should always pray and not give up" (Luke 18:1). As we read the Gospel accounts of His life, we see that Jesus prayed regularly (Luke 22:39), at times of decision making and crisis (Luke 22:39–44), when others were in need of a special miracle from God (Luke 9:15–17).

The apostle Paul wrote to the church at Thessalonica that we are to "pray continually" (1 Thessalonians 5:17). Prayer is communication with our heavenly Father, and if our relationship is close, our communication should take place regularly, frequently, and always be up-to-date.

Sometimes we think we can only pray in a certain place, like church or a quiet place in our home, with our eyes closed and our hands folded. Jesus gave us a different example. Jesus prayed wherever He went. The Bible says He prayed in the garden (Matthew 26:36), on a hillside (Matthew 14:23), along the way as He traveled with the disciples (Matthew 11:25). He prayed alone (John 6:15) and within large gatherings (Matthew 14:19). If we are to follow His example or the words of Paul and "pray continually," then we will pray wherever we are, any time of the day or night, with our eyes open or closed.

I remember as a young Christian I struggled with what it meant to pray continually. How is that possible when you are engaged in the heavy demands of home and work? As I matured in my relationship with Christ and in practicing my faith, I began to see this passage in a new way. Not as an unattainable goal as a believer but more a matter of attitude. I am to live my life in a spirit of prayer every day. As I begin my day talking with God, I allow Him to map out the important things to consider for the day. I lift up to Him the needs of those I know and those in my community and world that I do not know. As I move from this beginning-of-the-day conversation into an activity that requires more concentration, I simply put a comma as if there were only a pause in our conversation. At any given moment I can pick back up right where we left off with our conversation. This seems to me to be the spirit of Paul's advice when he said we are to pray continually. It is how we stay in close communication with God throughout the day.

Intercession

Miss Edna was considered a prayer advocate of the most committed kind in our church. She modeled for everyone what it meant to engage in intercessory prayer. Quietly and without a lot of fanfare, Miss Edna would start the prayer chain when a need arose. She always wrote down the request in a notebook and prayed until an answer came. She cared deeply about the people in our church and community. If she said she would pray for you, rest assured you were prayed for specifically and by name. She also prayed faithfully for missionaries serving in this country and around the world. She read everything she could about their work and their specific requests or needs for prayer. She served as the prayer coordinator for her missions group and kept everyone informed about many of the prayer needs and answers to prayers. She believed this was her calling, allowing her to partner with missionaries in ministry since she could no longer go herself due to her age and failing health.

I was one of those people that Miss Edna prayed for every day. She frequently asked where I would be traveling or what assignment I was working on. I knew she was asking because she wanted to be able to pray specifically for me. Sometimes on her way out of church on Sunday morning she would simply place her hand on my arm and smile. I knew that meant she would be praying for me. When Miss Edna died several years ago, I was told they found her in her room at the retirement center, lying peacefully in her bed with her Bible open and her hands folded as if in prayer. She demonstrated even in death what it meant to place prayer as a priority in her life and "pray continually."

Ministry

To understand the mission of God we need to be discipled in the importance of knowing Scripture and practicing a life of prayer modeled by Jesus. But Jesus also taught the disciples about ministering to others. Scripture tells us "Jesus went throughout Galilee, teaching in their synagogues, preaching the good news of the kingdom, and healing every disease and sickness among the people" (Matthew 4:23). We also hear Jesus' words calling us to become servants: "Whoever wants to become great among you must be your servant, and whoever wants to be first must be your slave—just as the Son of Man did not come to be served, but to serve, and to give his life as a ransom for many" (Matthew 20:26–28).

Jesus modeled with His own life what it meant to be a servant. He showed great sensitivity to those who were hungry. With a small amount of bread and fish, He performed a miracle that astounded the disciples in Matthew 14 and 15. When He came in contact with a man with leprosy, Jesus demonstrated His compassion for those with disabling illnesses. The disciples saw the importance of doing what was right versus what was considered appropriate for the culture of the day. He not only healed the man, but in doing so, He physically touched him (Matthew 8). He provided an example of ministering to others with compassion by healing the blind, the children, various women with mental and physical illnesses, and so many others.

Perhaps one of the most beautiful images of Christ's example as a servant is found in John 13 as Jesus performs what was considered to be the lowliest of tasks—washing the feet of someone else. As the evening meal was served, Jesus "took off his outer clothing, and wrapped a towel around his waist. After that, he poured water into a basin and began to wash the disciples' feet, drying them with the towel that was wrapped around him." When He finished washing every man's feet, He offered these words of explanation: "Do you understand what I have done for you? . . . You call me 'Teacher' and 'Lord,' and rightly so, for that is what I am. Now that I, your Lord and Teacher, have washed your feet, you also should wash one another's feet. I have set you an example that you should do as I have done for you. I tell you the truth, no servant is greater than his master, nor is a messenger greater than the one who sent him. Now that you know these things, you will be blessed if you do them" (John 13:4–5, 12–17). The visible message is clear and life-changing for the disciples then and now.

Several years ago, I had the opportunity to visit and work with the staff at the Graffiti center in lower Manhattan, a ministry in a neighborhood where many are homeless, suffering from drug and alcohol addiction, and where children are living with little supervision, much less a healthy family. For many years, volunteers have partnered with missionaries Taylor and Susan Field and others who work in this ministry. One day while visiting the center, I heard the story of a volunteer group who had been coming every winter for many years to perform a very special ministry for the homeless. At the beginning of winter, this group came with new shoes, socks, and supplies to perform foot care for these who live on the streets. They described how the group would pour basins of water and allow the people to soak their often dirty, crusted-over, callused feet in warm, soapy water. Then someone with medical knowledge would examine their feet for problems that required treatment and do what they could. They were each given new clean socks and shoes before returning to the streets of New York to survive another cold winter.

The image of these volunteers washing the feet of people from the streets of New York is forever imprinted in my mind next to the image of Christ washing the dirty, dusty feet of His disciples. He admonished all who were listening one day to feed the hungry, give drink to the thirsty, take in the stranger, clothe the naked, look after the sick and imprisoned. His words then, just as today, remind us that whatever we do "for one of the least of these brothers of mine," we do for the Lord (Matthew 25:40).

Discipleship is a process of learning God's Word, growing in our commitment to pray and to serve others like Jesus.

Gifted to serve

How can we learn to serve like Jesus when we feel we have nothing special to offer? Years ago at our church, my husband led a six-week course on discovering spiritual gifts. He invited anyone who wanted to know more to come to the first session. He assured the church that everyone had a spiritual gift, and they would leave the course with an awareness of what theirs might be and how it could be used in service to others. On the first evening, Pat came into the classroom and announced she was there to prove him wrong. She went on to say that she did not have any spiritual gifts; that she, in fact, didn't have any gifts or talents of any kind. She agreed to stay that night, and at the end of the first session, she heard enough to pique her interest. She came to the class each week, and by the end of the study, she agreed that she did in fact have a spiritual gift; she just didn't know what it was. She also left determined to discover it.

Several months went by and Pat's husband, a new Christian and an optometrist, volunteered for several missions trips to do eye clinics in the Caribbean. Pat agreed to help him prepare for the trips. She organized the eyeglasses and other supplies; she prepared the containers for shipping; and created assignments for team members. At the completion of the first trip, we all knew Pat had a spiritual gift. She was a very organized person who paid attention to details and offered her gift to meet the needs of others who lacked vision care.

Pat and her husband moved away some time after that, and we didn't see each other for many months. When we did meet at a convention, we asked about their new church and what kinds of things they were involved with in their new city. Pat laughed and reminded us of the spiritual gifts class and how she felt she didn't have any gifts. She thought spiritual gifts had to be something extraordinary and unusual. She began to tell us about her new role as director of the church's Sunday morning Bible study program. When they arrived at the church, the pastor shared a concern about how long it had been since someone provided leadership in this area of church life. The ministry was in disarray. He asked Pat if she would consider helping the church. She found through her experiences of organizing her husband's medical teams that she enjoyed bringing order to chaos. She applied those same skills to this new task, and now the entire program was flourishing.

As she found herself opening up to the possibility that God had indeed given her gifts, she felt a desire to learn to paint, and enrolled in a course at a college. She discovered a gift for putting on canvas the natural beauty of the places and memories of missions trips in which she and her husband participated. As we talked, without hesitation, she admitted God had indeed given her gifts, and she wanted to use them for His service. A few months later she presented our church with a beautiful painting of a scene from one of the islands where our church served on a volunteer medical missions experience with Pat and her husband. Pat is living proof that every one of us has a gift for service that brings pleasure to the Lord. Discovering those gifts is a part of the discipleship process as we grow as followers of Christ.

Live the Call

What is your spiritual gift? Do you believe you have at least one? When in doubt go back to Scripture for assurance that God has given you at least one. Spiritual gifts are discussed in various places in Scripture but the power to exercise those gifts in service was given as a promise from Jesus. Following the Crucifixion and Resurrection, Jesus knew His disciples would be devastated. He tried to prepare them for what was about to happen with words of encouragement and comfort. Words such as: "I will ask the Father, and He will give you another Counselor to be with you forever" (John 14:16); "I will not leave you as orphans; I will come to you" (John 14:18). Before ascending to heaven He gave them their instructions to teach all nations and to baptize them; and a promise, "Lo, I am with you always, even to the end of the age" (Matthew 28:20 NASB). And then, Jesus told them they would receive power to do the things they had observed and learned from him. It was the promise of the Holy Spirit (Acts 1:8).

What was true for the disciples is true for His followers today. When we commit all of ourselves to God, He sends His Holy Spirit to live within us, providing the power to live as His disciples. At the same time, He provides the unique gifts that are needed by each person to serve Him effectively. The apostle Peter said, "Each one should use whatever gift he has received to serve others, faithfully administering God's grace in its various forms" (1 Peter 4:10).

Paul taught the early churches what it means to be gifted for service. He acknowledged that each person has a specific calling, and their gifts, when contributed to the whole of the church, provide just what is needed to carry on the work of the church in the world. In Ephesians 4:12, Paul said we are given gifts "to prepare God's people for works of service, so that the body of Christ may be built up."

Chapter 12 of 1 Corinthians is often referred to as the "gifts" chapter. Paul reminded the people of the Corinthian church that there are different kinds of gifts and different forms of service. The giver of gifts is the Holy Spirit and each person receives at least one gift upon coming to faith in Jesus Christ. In 1 Corinthians 12:7, he stated the purpose of the gifts: "Now to each one the manifestation of the Spirit is given for the common good."

In her book *Uniquely Gifted*, Stuart Calvert affirms this biblical concept in her own life. She writes: "The Holy Spirit gives us gifts that enable us to honor and praise the Lord. He assigned us one or more gifts the day we were born again. He plans for us to use our gifts within a sphere of service."[3]

Discovering the gift or gifts God has given us is a part of the Christian journey of faith. If we fail to identify our gifts, we miss out on many blessings and opportunities for service. Working with teenagers for more than 25 years has given me numerous opportunities to see young people, young women in particular, discover their giftedness. Seeing teens teach children in a day camp or help a senior adult with a project then realize they have a gift for ministry is a priceless experience. The all-too-common "me-first" attitude that teens often exhibit disappears when they recognize their ability to do something for someone else.

On one missions project, I watched two girls who had been less than enthusiastic about working on a construction project change almost overnight. We were asked to help rebuild a church that was destroyed by torrential rains. We found ourselves deep in mud each day in the middle of a soybean field in Mississippi. Fortunately, the girls were assigned to work alongside a group of adult volunteers with construction experience. Instead of being relegated to menial work because they were girls, they found themselves being mentored in construction skills by a group of "grandpa" volunteer builders. They became energized as they learned how to apply insulation to the walls and were asked to nail down the flooring. They volunteered for backbreaking work once they saw the need and realized they could actually make a difference for this church. They found a special aptitude for learning new skills, and by the end of the week, they announced they would one day own their own construction business! I have no doubt they will do something incredible with their lives. It may not be a construction business, but what they learned that week will invariably influence their choices. They realized God gave them gifts they didn't know they had. They had a new awareness of His work in their lives and a renewed desire to serve Him.

Barbara Joiner, in her book *Yours for the Giving*, outlines many of the spiritual gifts found in Scripture and challenges us to recognize that we receive gifts through the work of the Holy Spirit at the moment we invite Christ into our lives. She reminds us: "Our gifts are given to us for a purpose. God gave us our gifts to give to others."[4]

Gifts versus fruit

Discipleship means we are learning and striving to become more like the One we are following. Jesus modeled for us the importance of Scripture, prayer, ministry, and using our gifts in service. But what is the difference between gifts of the spirit and fruit of the spirit? Stuart Calvert, in *Uniquely Gifted*, explains in simple terms: "Spiritual gifts equip Christians to minister, doing God's work in the world. The fruit of the spirit enables Christians to express the attitudes and to live the behavior that should accompany ministry in Jesus' name. The fruit is the medium through which the gifts are expressed." In other words, "Gifts define what a Christian does. Fruit defines who a Christian is."[5]

The evidence that discipleship is taking place is seen in a changed life; a life that is far different at the end of our days than when we began as an apprentice of Jesus Christ. Through our apprenticeship with Christ, His character should become our character. Discipleship is a journey of developing into a person whose life demonstrates the attributes Paul identified in Galatians 5 as the "fruit of the spirit." As we grow and mature in our faith, we will demonstrate the qualities of "love, joy, peace, patience, kindness, goodness, faithfulness, gentleness, and self-control" (Galatians 5:22–23) with increasing frequency. This fruit develops as we practice the things that were important to Christ. Reading the Bible and seeking to understand its teachings, committing ourselves to "praying continually," placing others first as we give ourselves in service, and using the gifts God has given us, will move us closer to the desired result of being a thoroughly discipled follower of Christ.

Discover truth

To understand God's mission in the world, we must first discover the truths for living found in the teachings of Jesus. We must become His apprentices. Only as we grow in our knowledge and understanding of His life will we begin to understand how we are to live as well. We are His disciples, called to disciple others while we are being discipled ourselves. Through the process of discipleship our minds become aligned with God's mission, our hearts become attuned to His call, and we find the courage and strength to live out that call each day.

Think about:

1. What does being a disciple mean?
2. How did Jesus choose the Twelve? How does God choose disciples today?
3. List the qualities of a disciple.
4. What does intercession mean? Who has interceded for you? Who should you be interceding for today?
5. What is the difference between gifts and fruit?
6. What are your gifts? What fruit do you produce?

CHAPTER 4

THE VIEW FROM ABOVE

"For God so loved the world that he gave his one
and only Son, that whoever believes in him shall
not perish but have eternal life."

John 3:16

I saw her in the airport in Washington, D.C. I was standing
in a long line of people waiting to check bags at the airline
desk. The computers crashed, and everything for this flight
had to be done by hand, so I observed her for a very long
time. She was struggling with two preschoolers (one of
which was most unhappy), a stroller, luggage, and a long
black veil that kept slipping off of her head. She tried to

soothe the child and replace the scarf over her face and head each time it slipped away. She needed a helping hand. I wanted to go; thought I should go, but I hesitated. I didn't want to lose my place in this long line. *I might miss my plane,* I told myself. *Besides, she is obviously not from America, and she might not speak English, so how could I help anyway? Surely someone will come along and help her . . . someone more like her!*

The truth is, I was uncomfortable approaching a woman whose face I could not see. So I hesitated, and I waited, and I hoped someone else would help her. After what seemed a long time, a man with dark hair and eyes and a very tanned complexion went over to her, said something I could not understand, took charge of the luggage, and walked away. She gathered the children and the stroller, readjusted her long wrap and black veil, and followed behind him into the evening crowd of the airport. I completed my check-in and hurriedly made my way to the departure gate. I was satisfied that someone had indeed come to the aid of this stranger in our land.

Some 48 hours later, after an overnight stop in London and having connected with the group I was to travel with, we were on the ground at our destination. Suddenly, it dawned on me as I put on my newly acquired long black coat and covered my own head with a scarf that I was becoming the stranger in a foreign land. During the next nine days there might be women who would observe me, and if I needed help, hesitate because I did not speak their language, because my coloring was different from theirs. I had a feeling God was about to teach me some valuable lessons.

We stepped off the plane into a world far different from any I had ever experienced. It was a world where Americans had not gone for many years because of conflict between our governments. My heart skipped a beat when I realized I was about to enter a country where Islam was the ruling authority and freedom had a different connotation than in America. We were there as tourists to visit the Old Testament ruins of what had been great palaces and communities in the days of Esther, Daniel, Nehemiah, Mordecai, and many more of the people I had only read about in the Bible. With a new ruler in control of the country, there was a slight opening to relationships with Americans. Eight of us, six of whom I had never met, were allowed to visit Susa and Persepolis and other ancient Persian ruins in this vast land. As we made our way through immigration and customs, the officials made copies of our passports and took their time in deciding whether or not to honor the visas we were granted. We became aware of our visitor status and were reminded how important it would be for us to obey their customs and laws, to be good tourists, if we hoped to pave the way for others to follow after us.

We had prepared for our trip by acquainting ourselves with the laws and culture of the land. We knew they prohibited alcohol, gambling, American movies and television, as well as many books from the West. We knew women, all women, must be covered from head to foot at all times with only hands and face showing when in public, and we agreed to honor their law. We knew that on a bus, in a restaurant, and in other public places as women we could not sit next to a man who was not our father, brother, or husband; so we were careful. We knew our demeanor in public needed to be reserved and respectful of their holy places. We would ask if and when we should remove our shoes and when we could take photos. We knew we would need permission to take a person's picture, and by our coming, we were agreeing to obey their laws of country and religion. So we were observant, opening our minds and our hearts to see what God saw in this land.

Over the course of nine days we were often reminded that we were strangers in a foreign land. We couldn't speak the language and few people could speak ours. We were in a foreign culture with much to learn. We were visitors in places of worship that felt strangely uncomfortable. It was a journey into a land where women and girls are not valued in quite the way I am used to. It felt strange to see them segregated at their places of worship, sitting huddled in the back of public buses, always covered in black from head to foot even in the desert areas with temperatures often above 105°F.

In the midst of much that I did not understand, there were some really great moments. The Old Testament came alive when we walked over the ruins that once was home to Esther and Mordecai, Nehemiah and Xerxes, Artaxerxes and Darius. We saw tombs where the rulers were buried in the side of a mountain. We saw elaborate carvings in the rock that told the history of a nation that once belonged to God and now were tourist attractions in a land that worshipped Muhammad. This trip could have been a simple tour of some ancient ruins. I could have returned home, shared my pictures with friends, and talked about how great it was to follow in Esther's footsteps in Susa and Persepolis. But I was keenly aware that God had another purpose in mind.

Scripture passages came to mind often as we traveled, passages reminding us of God's presence with us, His promise that all we had to do was ask and it would be granted, the challenge to His followers to be salt and light in a dark world. "You are the light of the world. A city on a hill cannot be hidden. Neither do people light a lamp and put it under a bowl. Instead they put it on its stand, and it gives light to everyone in the house" (Matthew 5:14–15). How could we shine brightly, I wondered, when it was forbidden to share Christ with the people we met? Then I remembered the freedom and privilege we have through prayer. And so we prayed as we walked the streets, rode the buses, and made our way across a land in need of God's presence and intervention. We also recognized His desire to change our hearts, our minds, so we could see the reality of life in the Muslim world. He called us to keep His purpose before us as we met people on the streets, in restaurants, in airports, always allowing His light to reflect through us.

The trip was not all grim and discouraging. There were unexpected blessings along the way as well. I discovered the women behind the veils were warm and beautiful, some of the most hospitable people I've ever met. Women in two different cities saw us not as strangers but as sisters and invited us into their homes. They asked about our culture, our faith, hugged us, served us, and provided a warm welcome not only to their homes but also into their hearts. At one point I realized the woman I was speaking with was a believer. I asked how she came to faith in a country where Christ is presented as a prophet and not God's Son, nor as the only way to salvation. She looked at me with a puzzled look and said: "Someone gave me a Bible. When I opened The Book and read His words, I heard His voice speaking to me telling me, 'I am the way, the truth and the life,' and I believed. Don't you hear His voice when you read The Book?" Standing in the midst of those who might cause her harm if they knew she was a follower of Christ, I was humbled beyond what words can express. We prayed as sisters in the Lord that evening with our eyes open and as if we were having a conversation. It was the sweetest time of prayer I have ever experienced.

Years later I can still see the faces of the people I met, their places of worship, and their homes. I remember the strangeness of their land and the sadness of knowing they do not know the "light" that has truly come through Jesus Christ. The experience changed my life and my perspective on the world. I see people differently, not as strangers to be afraid of, but as people God loves and for whom Christ died. I hear the evening news differently, my ears perking up with any news from this land. My heart is softer and more tender towards strangers in my own country, wondering how they feel about being in a strange culture, hearing a different language, eating different food, and then I remember.

Developing a worldview

What is your worldview? What in your life shapes your worldview? With what lens do you watch the news or read the newspaper? When you hear or read about injustice or persecution in other countries, what is the first thing that runs through your mind? Do you read past the headlines on these issues because they seem like abstract situations that will never affect you personally? What would happen if your view of the world and your understanding of Christian principles intersected in such a way that your responses to world situations were based on how Jesus would respond?

The answers to these questions might give you the beginning point to understanding more about your worldview. In a December 2003 news report, *worldview* was defined as a "term used to describe the belief system by which a person understands or makes decisions about the world."[1] Every person views the world from their own unique perspective based on their life experiences and exposure to a variety of teachings.

The results of a national survey conducted by Barna Research Group shows only 9 percent of Christians have a biblical worldview. The result of people not having a strong biblical worldview is seen in the way they live their lives. George Barna, the well-known Christian researcher, said, "The primary reason that people do not act like Jesus is because they do not think like Jesus. Behavior stems from what we think—our attitudes, beliefs, values, and opinions."

So how do we develop a biblical worldview? Where do we begin to allow God to shape our view of the world and how He wants us to think about the world? For our understanding and response to the needs of the world around us to be in line with how God sees them, we have to begin with our personal relationship with Christ. When we come to faith, we make choices about how or if we will grow and mature in our faith. We determine the influences around us and the time we are willing to commit to discovering God's design for our lives and for reaching His world with a message of hope through faith in Christ. No one can do it for us. We are each responsible for our own decisions.

Once a faith relationship is established, being discipled in our faith is critical. In the previous chapter, we looked at various ways Jesus discipled those around Him. In this chapter, we will look at growing in our understanding of Scripture, making prayer a regular part of our lives, discovering our gifts for ministry, and modeling that ministry after the ways Christ ministered.

God's desire for all nations

The starting place is always through a study of Scripture. Our view of the world is not God's view. We have a selfish personal view, but through Scripture we learn that God's view of the world has always included a focus on all the nations of the world. Think for a moment about God's plan for reaching all the nations.

From the time God told Abraham in Genesis 12:1–2 to "leave your country, your people and your father's household and go to the land I will show you" to the promise "I will make you into a great nation and I will bless you; I will make your name great, and you will be a blessing," God's desire to be made known among the nations was clear.

God repeated the promise to "bless the nations" through the descendants of Isaac in Genesis 26:3–4 and Jacob in Genesis 28:13–15. The covenant was repeated again in Genesis 35:9–12. God's promises to bless His people were always connected to His call for them to live as His children in relationship with a loving Father.

Numerous other Old Testament passages affirm that everything God did among His chosen people was to help make His name become known among those who did not know Him. David's victory over Goliath, for instance, provided an opportunity for people to learn about the presence and purposes of God. We read in 1 Samuel 17:46 that David killed Goliath "so the whole world will know that there is a God in Israel."

In 1 Chronicles 16:8, David himself acknowledged how the people were to make God "known among the nations, what he has done." Isaiah, Jeremiah, and the other prophets repeated over and over how God led His people to "make Him known among the nations."

The psalmist also refers to God and the nations. Psalm 67 reads, "may the nations be glad and sing for joy." Psalm 96:3 says it best, "Declare His glory among the nations, his marvelous deeds among all people."

God loves the world and all its people. He desires to have fellowship with all of His creation. Abraham was commissioned to reach all nations, and this commissioning continued on from one generation to the next of God's chosen leaders. God's focus on reaching the nations culminated in the coming of Christ. The bridge was built for all to come to Him. Jesus knew God's heart well. Therefore, His parting instructions to the disciples were to "go and make disciples of all nations" (Matthew 28:19). God's heart for the nations was revealed through the life of His Son and then through the disciples as they carried out the commission Christ gave them.

From Abraham to Jesus and finally to John's vision recorded in Revelation, God's heart for the nations of the world is clearly seen. John had a vision of the end of time, and he described it this way: "After this I looked and there before me was a great multitude that no one could count, from every nation, tribe, people, and language, standing before the throne" (Revelation 7:9).

To have a view of our world that matches God's view, we must begin with an understanding of Scripture. When we realize how important it is to God to be known among the nations, knowing more about Him and how to live our lives within His plan will become a priority.

Broadening our worldview

Living in a culture that is so focused on "me" and "mine" makes it difficult to see the world as God sees it. We must make an intentional effort to shift the heavy focus off of ourselves and our needs. We need to remember the priorities that Christ taught when He quoted Deuteronomy 6. We have to love God first with all we have, love others second, and then have a healthy love for ourselves as a part of God's creation.

Once we have studied Scripture and realigned our priorities with God's, a very practical way to develop our view of the world is to develop and feed our curiosity about the world and its people with accurate information and experiences. We need to venture outside our own known and comfortable world.

A vast amount of information about the world is at our fingertips. Many books and articles reporting current happenings in our world are readily available to us. However, the Internet has become the most frequently used resource for finding information about world events, changes in world trends, and basic needs of people groups around the world. Just by typing in the name of a country, or people group, you will find thousands of pages of information that bring the world right to your home.

Lack of information is not the problem. It is the lack of curiosity or interest in knowing about the world that has become the obstacle. When we are focused on "me," we have no time to develop an interest in world events. We must first decide it is important to be exposed to information about our world before we will make learning about our world a priority.

To encourage a biblical worldview, we must intentionally and consistently expose ourselves to accurate information about world events and cultures different from our own. In the context of church, being part of a small group where the focus is on world events, biblical principles related to responding to world needs, and discussions about how to minister cross-culturally helps to provide a lasting effect on our thought processes and behavior. Through regular, ongoing exposure to information from around the world, sought individually or within a missions-minded group, we are able to change the way we see the world and discover God's view more clearly.

Personal experiences also change the way we view the world. As you drive around your city or town, do you see places of worship other than Protestant and Catholic? Are there temples or mosques? Have you ever visited these or contacted someone you know who attends and asked if you could visit? Are there ethnic restaurants, shops, or neighborhoods where you live? Opening our eyes to those around us and developing a curiosity about what they believe and their background will broaden our view of God's world.

We live in a very travel-friendly world. A growing trend for churches and individuals is to participate in a missions trip each year. It is a good practice to set aside time to leave home and focus entirely on one area of ministry for a period of time. We can learn so much by being personally involved.

Many people travel around the world with their jobs. So often, though, when we travel for work we have tunnel vision about the purpose of the trip. We stay in our hotels and never venture out into the community while we are there. One of my favorite things to do wherever I travel is to go to the local grocery store. You can learn a lot by seeing what is available in the local market. I usually bring home the local coffee or tea and whatever sweet cookie or candy they have that is made locally. I save some of these special treats for Christmas. My family says every Christmas is like taking a trip around the world, as they delve through the simple, common items I have picked up for them. As you travel, be curious about the people and the place you are visiting.

Sipping coffee in a local coffee shop is another way to educate ourselves about new cultures. Watching people, listening to conversations even when you can't understand the words, and sampling local food is an education. Walking through the local shopping district, not the tourist shops, reveals a great deal about the economic condition and the lifestyle of many of the community's people. Nurture a spirit of curiosity about the world and your worldview will grow.

Opening our eyes

Study of Scripture, aligning ourselves with God's priorities to love Him first and others second, and a curiosity about the things that God cares about will help broaden our view of the world. But if we are serious about seeing the world as God sees it, the most important element is to ask God to open our eyes so that we may clearly see the truths He is trying to develop within us.

The Old Testament story of Elisha is one of a man who desired more than anything to serve God effectively following in the footsteps of Elijah. As he matured in his ability to lead and perform miracles, a time of great testing came. In 2 Kings 6, we read where the king of Aram sent his soldiers to capture Elisha. Elisha's servant became afraid and ran to Elisha and asked what they should do. Beginning in verse 16 we read Elisha's response: "'Don't be afraid,' the prophet answered. 'Those who are with us are more than those who are with them.' And Elisha prayed, 'O LORD, open his eyes so he may see.' Then the LORD opened the servant's eyes, and he looked and saw the hills full of horses and chariots of fire all around Elisha" (2 Kings 6:16–17).

God's presence and powerful provision of protection was all around them and prevented the enemies from capturing Elisha. The problem was the servant couldn't see them until Elisha asked God to open his eyes.

We can learn something from Elisha about how we see the world. If we truly want God's view of the world to become ours, we must ask Him to open our eyes so we can see what He wants us to see. But be careful when you pray— God will answer, and once you see, there's no going back to your small, narrow view of the world.

New perspectives

I have traveled to many places around the world—the Caribbean, Latin America, Asia, Europe, and I have even lived for a year in another country. My first visit into the world of Islam, however, changed my view of the world in a dramatic fashion unlike any other experience. If I had only followed the planned path for tourists and never allowed my eyes and my heart to venture into the real world of the people by observing, listening, and asking questions, I would have missed the reason God had me there. By stepping out of my fear of the unknown and accepting invitations into the homes of the local people, I gained a new perspective about what life is like for those who live behind the veil.

Each of us needs to look around the places where we live, places we travel, and materials we have access to for a worldwide education and take advantage of all the opportunities God places before us. Let's look out into the world unafraid of what we might find and allow God to shape our view of the world into His view. When we allow that to happen, we will begin to understand God's mission in the world and discover how we fit into His great plan.

Think about:

1. Do people of different cultures and lifestyles live near you? How do you react when you see these people?
2. How can you reach out to people who are different from you?
3. Do you use the Internet to learn about other countries? What are other ways you can learn about cultures and lifestyles of God's children?
4. What keeps people from reaching out to others? What keeps you from reaching out to neighbors in your community who have different lifestyles than yours?
5. How can you broaden your view of the world?

Section 2

Embrace
the Mission of God

Jesus calls us o'er the tumult
Of our life's wild restless sea;
Day by day His sweet voice soundeth,
Saying, "Christian, follow Me!"

Jesus calls us from the worship
Of the vain world's golden store,
From each idol that would keep us,
Saying, "Christian, love Me more."

The Baptist Hymnal (1991 edition)

Cecil Alexander was a famous hymn writer in the late nineteenth century. He wrote the words to this familiar hymn, capturing the heart of what it means to embrace God's call in our lives. The word *embrace* implies that something is accepted willingly and gladly as one's own. To embrace the mission of God means we understand God's heart and purpose in the world. We see more clearly what He wants to do in our lives and how He wants us to be a part of His mission. We willingly accept His call to the work, striving to live out that call in His power each day.

We will face challenges when we decide to embrace God's call. One of the most prevalent challenges will be to discover what to move out of our lives to make room for His call. There may be many things and activities that need to be moved out of first place in our lives so we can follow God's call. We must be ever watchful of ways to grow in our understanding of God's design for stewardship.

When we embrace the mission of God, our personal response time to His call will be shortened because we have become aware of the world around us and we are ready and willing to go next door, down the street, across the sea, whenever and wherever He leads.

Chapter 5

Make Room in Your Life

"God does not call us to find out where we are. He already knows. He is calling each one to trust Him personally. And when we answer, He will make a difference in our lives."

Janet Hoffman, *God Is Calling You*[1]

Janet Hoffman is a special friend of mine who has served most of her life in ministry with her husband. As a pastor's wife, teacher, church leader, and former president of Woman's Missionary Union® (WMU®), Janet demonstrates what it means to understand and embrace God's design for her life. She is on a lifelong journey of growing in her faith and listening for God's voice. God uses various ways to touch our lives with His love and His call. For Janet, one special relationship started it all.

As a little girl, Janet spent several weeks in the summer with her grandparents. Her grandfather was a minister and often preached revivals during the summertime. Janet enjoyed a very special relationship with him. On one of her visits he preached a sermon titled "The Call of God," based on John 11:28 where Martha told her sister, Mary, "The Teacher is here and is asking for you." Following the service, her grandfather simply asked Janet if God was calling her to trust Him so He could make a difference in her life. Several weeks later Janet knew God was indeed calling her to faith. She knew as a child that her encounter with Christ was real because suddenly her thoughts and her actions were different; she wanted to obey her parents, to tell the truth, speak kind words with her friends. She felt loved in a special way and became more sensitive to the teachings of the Bible. Janet began the journey of discipleship and was baptized later by her grandfather.

On a subsequent visit to see her grandparents, Janet learned that God's call is not only a call to faith but also a call to follow Christ into the world. After meeting a missionary for the first time, her grandfather taught her about God's love for all the people of the world. He exposed her to new ideas and a view of the world from God's vantage point.

In *God Is Calling You*, Janet relates the teachings she learned from this saintly grandfather:

You can be sure that God is calling. So listen for His call

To trust Him as personal Savior;

To learn about Him and His plan for the world to love Him;

To serve Him in your daily Christian life; and

To do your part in His great missions plan:

By praying for missionaries; giving to missions offerings, and doing missions projects right where you live; or

By being a missionary sent to another state or country to show and tell the story of Jesus and His love.

Since that day, Janet says, "I have known that God is calling me. Some days I listen better than others. But when I take time to stay very close to Him through daily Bible reading and praying, I listen carefully for His call. And then, I know it is true: As incredible as it may seem, God is calling me."[2]

Following God's call

God's call has taken Janet in many different directions. She acknowledges that God calls us to "do different things at different times" in our lives but always with a passion for seeing the world come to know Christ. Her life is an example of what it means to understand God's mission in the world and embrace the plan that He created just for her. Janet and I have spent countless hours together traveling, sharing our hearts about God's desires for our families and the organization we both love and serve. She is a woman who believes deeply in prayer and rises early in the morning to spend special time with God, seeking His will for her life for that day. Because of her faithfulness to follow God's call since her grandfather first introduced her to the truth that God is calling each of us, many have come to faith, and the mission of God has advanced.

Janet, like so many of us, repeatedly examines her priorities and makes choices all along the way that help keep her focused on God's call for her life. It doesn't happen easily or without a consistent, intentional focus on following God's plan. In an earlier chapter, I identified some potential roadblocks to living the call of God in our lives: hurry sickness, a culture of "meism," and a growing cynicism about organized religion. There are many others that we could identify but the challenge is the same. To understand God's mission and embrace His specific call for our lives requires an intentional decision on our part. We are the ones who decide if we will seek His direction, listen for His voice, and ultimately make the decision to follow. Only we can lay aside the busyness of our days and make room for God and His plan.

Ruth and Naomi

Scripture teaches us that making room for the things of God, moving roadblocks out of our way so we can follow God's plan, is not a new challenge. The story of Ruth and Naomi is a perfect example of the difficult choices that may come our way as we seek to embrace God's design for our lives.

Some of the most familiar verses in the Bible, often repeated at weddings, are found in the Book of Ruth. "Don't urge me to leave you or to turn back from you. Where you go I will go, and where you stay I will stay. Your people will be my people and your God my God" (Ruth 1:16). These verses highlight Ruth's heartfelt desire when she was confronted with a choice that would alter her future forever.

Naomi had married Elimelech years before, and they were blessed with two sons. A famine occurred in the land, and they left Judah for a better place, Moab. Unfortunately, Elimelech died leaving Naomi a widow with two children. Naomi remained in Moab, and after a time her sons married Moabite women. Ten years later, Naomi grieved again when both sons died. In a culture where a woman is only valued if attached to her father, husband, or sons, Naomi must have been devastated. How could she take care of herself much less her daughters-in-law without a male supporter? After hearing that God prepared a way for people in Judah to have food, she decided to return to her homeland.

Naomi obviously cared deeply for her daughters-in-law. The Scripture says "they wept aloud" (Ruth 1:9) as she instructed them to return to their homes to their mothers where they might have a better life, be able to marry again, and have a future. Orpah grudgingly followed Naomi's request, but Ruth could not bring herself to leave Naomi. She spoke those very familiar words found in verse 16, pledging her support, care, and love for Naomi and the God of Naomi. She returned with Naomi to a place she did not know and to an uncertain life, but Ruth placed her trust in the God she had come to know through Naomi. These two women faced serious challenges—a lack of basic life necessities, cultural barriers, religious differences, grief over the loss of family as well as the comfort of a known lifestyle. But they chose to put God first, each other second, and trusted God to provide for them as individuals. They embraced what seemed to be God's design for the next steps in their life. And God was faithful, bringing Boaz into their lives with a new home and a new family.

Through Ruth and Naomi's example, we are challenged to move things out of our lives that might surface as roadblocks and prevent us from hearing His voice. Ruth made room for God when she had little evidence that her life would be any better. She stepped out in faith without knowing the end result. She embraced God's plan, and He rewarded her faithfulness with His presence and protection.

Stepping out

Several years ago, Debby called me with the news that she and her husband had made a radical decision. Having lived most of their lives in the Northeast, they were moving south. To say I was surprised would be putting it mildly. Debby and I have been friends for a long time. We discovered early in our friendship that we have much in common through our roles as wives, mothers, and now as grandmothers. We're both nurses who discovered a vocational calling early and practiced this one profession throughout adulthood. Out of our common love for missions, we have spent many years as volunteers helping equip people with an understanding of how God works in our world and calls us to embrace our own unique place of service. Much of our volunteer service has been through the organization I now lead, which is how we met. But there is one thing we do not share—a common culture. She is very much from the northern US culture, and I have spent most of my years in the South. But what fun the difference has made in our relationship! Debby introduced me to clam chowder and taught me how to navigate snow, while I took her by subway in Atlanta, Georgia, to introduce her to fried green tomatoes. God gave us a special gift when He made this southern girl and a girl from New Hampshire spiritual sisters and friends.

One of the qualities I most admire about Debby is her spiritual depth. She is a woman deeply committed to prayer. She practices what Jesus taught us about meeting the needs of people and relying on the power of prayer. I knew she did not make this decision to move south easily, nor without much prayer. What she shared with me about her journey, from denying God's call to embracing His call, reminded me of the importance of allowing God to move things out of our lives so we can make room for His call.

Debby's story

"God has extended a variety of calls on my life: the call to become His child through the grace gift of salvation; the call to deny myself and live for Christ; the call to step out in faith into leadership; the call to personal ministry in a multihousing neighborhood. The most recent God call on my life was to move away from our home of 30 years in New Hampshire, away from our child and her family, and away from the only lifestyle I had ever known. God called my husband, Brad, and me to journey into the unknown with Him and to discover the place He planned for us in the South to live and to serve. Where that would be, we didn't know. We simply knew He would reveal it to us one step at a time.

"When Brad first told me how God was speaking to him about His plan for us to move south, I was certain Brad had it wrong. I was angry at Brad's peaceful acceptance of this radical idea. Brad calmly suggested I pray about it. Pray I did. I walked . . . actually trudged up and down our hilly roads over many days, telling God how He needed to explain to Brad that this wasn't, just couldn't be, His plan for our lives.

"God listened, and then one day said, 'You are fighting Me, not Brad. I want you to go.' It was God's voice. I could only submit. God gave me this verse: Isaiah 43:18–19, 'Forget the former things; do not dwell on the past. See I am doing a new thing! Now it springs up; do you not perceive it?'

"Some did not believe God would really call us to live in another place. I heard, 'It's not as if you are being sent to a missions field.' And I was asked, 'Do you really think God would send you to the Bible Belt when there are so many lost people here in New England?' Some were angry. I wondered if they feared God would ask them to leave what was so dear to them.

"Our daughter was sad, taking a long time to accept this and wondering what she would do if she needed me right away. We left behind our daughter and her family, aging parents, brothers and sisters, friends of 30 years, the home we built, our wonderful church family, our places of service, and the beauty of New England.

"God has the right to interrupt and redirect our lives at any moment. God's call may initially feel risky, but His call is filled with assurance of His faithfulness, of His trust in us to heed the call. Not answering God's call is what is truly risky and unsafe. God's call always is to an adventure and an adventure I never want to miss. In this call I was challenged to trust God's plan when, like Abraham and Sarah, we did not know to what land God would take us. Together we have faced the challenges of putting down roots in a new place, of making 'home' in the place God would take us, of resting in God's understanding and not our own. We have faced the challenges of accepting God's purposes for our new life in our new community, not knowing if God would take us down familiar paths of missions or lead us in new directions for service.

"But, ah, the result! Perfect peace! An awesome adventure with God! Wonderful new friends! A missions-hearted church! Ministry together in our new life! The incomparable joy of being in God's will!"

Step-by-step

God's call may not always be understood at first nor accepted by our friends and family. If our focus becomes so strong on pleasing those around us, we could lose sight of God's calling. In Debby's case, the comfort of a known lifestyle, family, and the questioning of friends could have become roadblocks keeping her from knowing the joy of embracing God's new call. Despite her fear and initial feelings of uncertainty, Debby committed to pray and seek God's will. She demonstrated a willingness to trust God's Word and have faith in His love for her, knowing He always seeks the best for her life. Because she intentionally moved her roadblocks out of the way, she and Brad are experiencing great joy in serving God in the South.

Frederick Buechner, in the book *Wishful Thinking: A Theological ABC*, says, "The place God calls you to is the place where your deep gladness and the world's deep hunger meet."[3] God's voice comes to us when we genuinely seek His will for our lives. He knows the place of greatest need for the gifts and abilities within each of us. When we ask for His direction, He will answer. It may not be the answer we want, but Debby's testimony reminds us of the importance of listening and following step-by-step until we can embrace God's direction and the place He has for our lives.

The woman at the well

John 4 is the story of a different kind of woman. Unlike Debby, this woman did not seek God's direction and therefore, made the wrong choices all her life. Whatever the roadblocks were to her knowing and understanding God's plan for her life, she gave in to them rather than embracing God's design. Scripture reveals that one bad decision led to another until she was caught in a vicious cycle of immorality and hopelessness. Used by men and shunned by women, she avoided the crowds and even the fellowship of neighbors. She came out to do her chores at noontime because she assumed all the neighborhood women would be at home avoiding the heat. She hoped by avoiding the women, she would not have to endure their whispers and disapproving looks.

One day when she ventured out for water, there was a man at the well who asked her for a drink. She was shocked, to say the least, that a man, a Jewish man at that, would even speak to her, a mere woman. Also, as a Samaritan, she was part of the most despised ethnic group of her day. Jews and Samaritans did not speak to one another much less share a drink of water. A dialogue began, and before long, she realized this Jew knew all about her life, and yet He didn't condemn her. It must have been the first time in many years that she felt like a real person, someone of worth and value. As He listened to her, He simply confronted her with the truth. He challenged her to seek a better way and pointed her in the right direction. But the choice was hers.

Through an intentional decision on her part to remain at the well, to talk with this man who she perceived to be a prophet, her life took a dramatic turn. Through His offer of "living water," Jesus demonstrated for her what it meant to experience God's love and forgiveness. Because of His words and the kindness with which He presented them, her roadblocks to faith dissolved, and she believed. So great was her transformation, Scripture tells us she left her water pot at the well and ran to tell the townspeople about Jesus. She must have appeared noticeably different and bold in her witness because John 4:39 says, "Many of the Samaritans from that town believed in Him because of the woman's testimony."

A daily process

Author and minister James R. Kok said, "Faith is the capacity to trust God while not being able to make sense out of everything."[4] Janet, Ruth and Naomi, Debby, and the woman at the well exercised faith when God called them, even though it may not have made sense at the time. At some point they each must have understood that God loved them, that He had a design for their lives that was just right for them. They each came to a crossroads where they had to make a decision—to trust God's call and embrace it or go their own way, risking the loss of God's best for their lives.

We face those same decisions as well. When we are already so busy with so many good things, it seems impossible to add one more thing to our lives. That's when we need to step back, reevaluate how we are spending our time, energy, resources, and listen for God's call. We need to ask God and ourselves what we need to move out of our busy lives so we can hear the call of God to the more important things. It is a dilemma we all will face at one time or another if we are truly seeking God's direction.

Billy Graham wrote that "being a Christian is more than just an instantaneous conversion—it is a daily process whereby you grow to be more and more like Christ."[5] How can we remove the roadblocks to understanding and embracing God's call so we can fulfill His plan for our lives? It begins with an intentional seeking on our part, asking God in prayer for His plans for our day, for His will regarding how we spend our time. We ask God to help us move our focus from thinking only about ourselves to thinking His thoughts, to hearing His voice instead of the voices of those who would pull us down into a world of negative thoughts and actions.

Jesus said: "Ask and it will be given to you; seek and you will find; knock and the door will be opened to you. For everyone who asks receives; he who seeks finds; and to him who knocks, the door will be opened" (Matthew 7:7–8). What a great promise as we ask God to help us make room in our lives for the things that matter most.

Think about:

1. When did you first hear God's call?
2. How can you tell God is calling you?
3. What does it mean to embrace God's plan for your life?
4. How did Ruth embrace God's plan? What happened when she did?
5. Are you embracing God's plan for your life? In what ways?

Chapter 6

Who Owns It?

"God normally calls us along the line of our giftedness, but the purpose of giftedness is stewardship
and service, not selfishness."

Os Guinness, *The Call*[1]

I can't remember the first time I heard the Brooklyn
Tabernacle Choir perform. Their name is synonymous with
passionate, energetic worship. At first glance a person might
assume this is one of those success stories of a megachurch
that never had to struggle to reach its potential. But under-
neath the dynamic music of a choir lies the story of God's
faithfulness in meeting the needs of His church when His
people follow His call.

Jim Cymbala, in his book *Fresh Wind, Fresh Fire*, describes one of his earliest encounters with God's call in his life.[2] As a young businessman in Manhattan, he married the daughter of a minister. They were both believers in Christ and had a desire to serve Him but understood their place to be the crazy New York marketplace. They, like many others in New York City, were on a fast track to success and financial security. But God had other plans and used Jim's father-in-law to encourage him in the direction of pastoral ministry. After surviving the first year as pastor of a small church in Newark, New Jersey, Jim was asked to preach on Sunday evenings at an inner-city, multiracial church in Brooklyn. On his first evening he found a discouraged young pastor, a chaotic worship service, as well as a small and most unusual assortment of people. Within a few weeks the pastor resigned, attendance was down to a handful, someone accused an usher of stealing from the offering plate, and Jim found himself suddenly responsible for two small struggling congregations. Burning the candle at both ends best describes the life he and his wife, Carol, were living as they tried to keep both congregations functioning.

Jim struggled with whether or not God had actually called him to pastor, much less address the severe needs of a church in the midst of a community of drug addicts, poverty, materialism, and a host of different cultural backgrounds. The day came when he had to choose between the two churches: devote full time to the one in New Jersey that actually paid him a modest salary or turn his energy to the one that could not even pay its own mortgage payments, much less provide him with a salary. But he and Carol both knew God was calling them to serve in Brooklyn. They took second jobs and made the commitment to serve Brooklyn Tabernacle Church.

Serving as pastor of this church became one of the most difficult challenges they ever faced as a couple. At one of Jim's lowest moments, when confronted with an illness that would not heal and feeling totally inadequate as a pastor, Jim confessed his deep feelings of inadequacy to God. With tears flowing at this deeply critical juncture in his life, he experienced God's presence and heard Him speak deep in his soul. He knew beyond a shadow of a doubt that if the Brooklyn Tabernacle Church were to survive, they would have to commit themselves to earnestly pray and seek God's heart. Only God could help them become the church in the city that He would use to transform lives and the entire community. Tuesday night prayer meetings became the most important service of the week. Individuals in the church came to authentic faith and others recommitted their lives to the Lord. They began to minister to hurting people in their midst and God began to build His church. He gave the people a song of praise in their hearts, and before long, the Brooklyn Tabernacle Choir emerged and began to share their song with all who would listen.

Jim and Carol Cymbala, an ordinary couple, sought to live the good life in New York. Since they never trained for the ministry, God's call came as a surprise to both of them. But because of their willingness to hear His call, to step out in faith and give God all that they had, they found great joy in embracing God's design for their lives. They discovered the greatest pathway to success was through prayer. They learned what it meant to be good stewards of God's gifts by persistently focusing their attention on God's desires instead of their own. As a result, countless thousands of people have entered into God's kingdom through the testimony of the Brooklyn Tabernacle Church and its choir.

Rabbi Bernard Raskas says, "God does not want us to do extraordinary things; he wants us to do ordinary things extraordinarily well."[3] When God calls us to something we have not been trained to do, and we feel inadequate to serve, Jim would remind us that if we first give it all to God, He is sufficient to provide for our every need. More than that, He has promised to walk with us through the valleys as well as on the mountaintop of success. What God requires is submission of all that we have and are to His purposes. He takes whatever we offer and makes the ordinary, extraordinary, multiplying it for His sake.

Understanding stewardship

Some who read the story of the Brooklyn Tabernacle Church might say in the early days, the church experienced a stewardship issue. They couldn't pay their bills, provide a livable salary for their pastor, nor plan for their future building needs. To be a viable ministry in a city the size of New York, they needed someone to educate them about tithing and giving offerings to God. They needed a funds consultant to analyze their neighborhood and help develop a plan to draw in people with money. In many churches this might be true, but usually the problem goes deeper than a lack of money; it is a lack of understanding that God already owns everything and is simply waiting for us to give back to Him what is rightfully

His. It is more than a money issue; it is a stewardship of life issue.

What is your understanding of stewardship? Is it giving money to your church? Is it giving an extra gift to a special charity at the end of the year? Neither of these is bad; but if the only concept we have of stewardship is related to money, then we have missed some important biblical truths. In his book *Trusted Steward*, Calvin Partain states that "a steward is a manager of goods that belong to someone else."[4] He outlines three basic foundational truths of stewardship:

1. God owns everything.
2. God has entrusted some of His possessions to us.
3. God holds us accountable.

These simple truths call us to recognize that God, the Creator of all of life, has entrusted us with everything we are and have—our body, mind, soul, talents, time, and possessions. The Greek word for *entrusted* is translated "to deliver to one something to keep, use, take care of, manage." God has graciously given each of us many wonderful gifts and abilities. His desire is that we use those in service for Him. As we exercise our giftedness, God's call and how we are to live that call emerges.

There were many times in Scripture when Jesus addressed stewardship. One of those times is found in Matthew 25. Jesus presented the story of three men given varying amounts of talents, an equivalent of our money. The first two found ways to multiply the talents bringing back to the owner twice what he had given them for safe keeping. In both instances the Master said: "Well done, good and faithful servant! You have been faithful with a few things; I will put you in charge of many things. Come and share your master's happiness!" (Matthew 25:23).

But the third servant buried his talent and did not use it productively. When the master returned, all he could do was dig it up, present his excuses for doing nothing, and give it back. The master was not pleased to say the least. He called the man a "wicked, lazy servant" (v. 26) and threw him "outside, into the darkness" (v. 30).

What can we draw from this parable of Jesus? At first glance it may seem harsh or insensitive on the part of the master. We probably remember times when we have been fearful, afraid of trying something and failing. When we think about what we each have in the way of gifts, abilities, resources, time, and money, this passage encourages us to use all of it in whatever way we can. God gives each of us different gifts. The more we use what He has given us, the better we become at exercising the gift or managing the time. Those of us who took piano lessons as children learned the value of practicing or the sad reality of not practicing. How many of us cannot play a piano today because we failed to use the talent when it was fresh?

The master rewarded the two men who made good use of their talents. They were given more and received great affirmation from him. So it is with God's children as well. Calvin Partain says, "God pays faithful stewards well. In this life, they have a sense of purpose and accomplishment. "The secret to successful stewardship is found in switching from our power to God's power!"[5] If we are sensitive to His call and follow, in the next life we too will hear Him say, "well done, good and faithful servant" (Matthew 25:21). The more we trust Him with what He has given us, the more He trusts us and allows us to participate in His design for reaching the world.

Business to ministry

Owen Cooper was a businessman from Yazoo City, Mississippi. He was a man of vision and one who believed in making the best of himself through education. He received his undergraduate degree in agriculture from Mississippi State University and a master's degree in economics and political science from the University of Mississippi. He later received a law degree. He was a lifelong learner in the truest sense. As an agriculturist, he created his own company, the Mississippi Chemical Company, a large fertilizer business. Once the company was well established, he worked at the company four hours a day and then spent the other four hours focusing on how to meet the needs of the world. He believed strongly that God wanted him to make a difference in the world beyond Mississippi. Through his church, he participated in missions projects around the world and used his skills as a businessman to minister to others.

The story is told that on a trip to India he was confronted with rampant starvation. He believed in helping people help themselves. He knew he could rally donated food supplies for the people, but for how long? The best approach was to help the Indian people raise their own level of food production. To do that, he recognized their need for fertilizer—the one thing he knew the most about. Through a lengthy process, Owen Cooper helped the nation of India build the largest fertilizer plant in the world; larger than his own,

which had been supplying India with 250,000 tons of fertilizer a year.

Today India is an exporter of food to other countries in
need of assistance. What kind of man cuts his own profits in
business by helping people become self-sufficient? Many in
the business world would not understand his way of doing
business. He was the kind of man who wanted to make a difference; one who understood the meaning of being a steward
of all that God had entrusted to him. This included his education, his business expertise, his time, and his personal
resources. He took the talents God gave him and invested
them in the lives of other people rather than keep them for
himself. As he worked alongside the Indian people, he also
recognized their need for Christ. He was instrumental in
helping those with whom he worked come to know Christ
and develop into people of influence among their own for
Christ. Owen Cooper understood that "the purpose of giftedness is stewardship and service, not selfishness" and incor-
porated that concept into his lifestyle.

Catching a vision

The more we travel around the world, the more we see
people with so little accomplishing so much. Being a good
steward doesn't always mean people have a wealth of
resources to offer, but they are using whatever they have to
accomplish something God has called them to. In
Zimbabwe, Africa, a group of 14 women, living in poverty,
caught a vision for helping their group of believers build
their very own church. Despite terrible economic conditions
in their country, they began making craft items such as cro-

cheted doilies, candle holders, maracas—whatever they could make with natural resources available to them. They used their first earnings to build a toilet facility for the church; next, they built a security wall. This year, they hope to provide resources for actually building the church . They understand that whatever God has given them is to be used to bring Him glory. Their vision is paying off in tangible ways for their church.

A young woman in the Middle East discovered she had a talent for sewing small, colorful saddles for wooden camel figurines; the money she earned enabled her to attend and graduate from college. When asked if she would stop sewing since she achieved her scholastic goal, she said no; her brothers needed an education, and she would continue using her talent to fund their education as well.

In South Africa, Siggi, a Christian woman inspired by Ephesians 4:28, dared to believe that God could use her gift for sewing to lead others to Christ. She started a ministry called Wezandla, which means "hands" in Zulu. Today 300 women are meeting for Bible study and working part-time in the ministry. Six others are working full-time as sewers. Most of these exist in poor economic conditions, living in clay huts without running water or electricity. Many are illiterate and have several children to care for. Because of God's call on Siggi's life, they are learning about Christ and finding hope for a better way of life.

These people and many more have found an outlet for items they make through a ministry called WorldCrafts℠. Started by WMU in 1996, this ministry evolved because God called women to find creative ways to introduce the message of the gospel among the poor in their village. Over the years, WorldCrafts has seen tremendous growth. Through Bible study and prayer, crafting and fellowship, many in over 26 regions of the world have found a way to earn a living and feed their families. Through WorldCrafts, they also hear a message of hope about a God who loves them and a Savior who gave His life for them. They too have learned that "the purpose of giftedness is stewardship and service, not selfishness."

Gifted to work

At a luncheon recently, everyone in the room was asked to stand, tell our name, and tell what we do professionally. Someone stood and said, "I am an attorney for . . ." Another person stated she was a professor at a local university. And another said she was a nurse. For many of us, our work defines us; we believe we are what we do. Os Guinness, in *The Call*, states: "Work, for most of us, determines a great part of our opportunity for significance and the amount of good we are able to produce in a lifetime. Besides, work takes up so many of our waking hours that our jobs come to define us and give us our identities. . . . A sense of calling should precede a choice of job and career, and the main way to discover calling is along the line of what we are each created and gifted to be. Instead of, 'You are what you do,' calling says: 'Do what you are.'"[6]

At some point in our lives, many of us make decisions about our choice of vocation. If we believe God already owns everything, and we are stewards of all He gives us, we should also believe God desires to work in and through us, using our gifts and abilities in every aspect of our lives, including our vocations.

The prophet Jeremiah reminds us that God has a plan for our lives: "'For I know the plans I have for you,' declares the Lord, 'plans to prosper you and not to harm you, plans to give you hope and a future. Then you will call upon me and come and pray to me, and I will listen to you. You will seek me and find me when you seek me with all your heart'" (Jeremiah 29:11–13). God wants to help shape our choices about how we will spend our time and our energy through whatever avenue of work we choose.

Kay Bennett serves among the poor and hurting in the French Quarter of New Orleans. Growing up on a dairy farm in rural Mississippi, Kay knew the love and support of family and church. She went to college sensing that God wanted her work in a "helping profession." While earning a degree in counseling and psychology, she did an internship at a mental health facility. In the midst of meeting the emotional and physical needs of people, she realized something was missing in her work. She became uncomfortable and sensed God was calling her to do more. It wasn't enough as a Christian to just meet physical needs; God wanted all she had to offer.

In an interview, Kay said, "To not be able to minister to the spiritual need made me feel limited and feel like I had left the most important part out. This is when I knew God was calling me to a ministry in which I could minister to the whole person."

Kay talked with her pastor and other Christian leaders about her calling. She heard about a program where she could study towards a degree in Christian counseling and enrolled in a seminary. Kay said she knew this was right because "I found the peace that Paul talks about; a peace that passes all understanding. God opened the door for me to be a missionary in New Orleans and to minister to the homeless. It is everything I ever wanted to do. I am able to minister to the whole person. I found a home with the homeless."

But fulfilling her call did not come without its challenges. When Kay tried to secure city permission to convert an existing ministry building to overnight housing for homeless women and children, the city balked. Many people told her to give up, but God would not release her from this part of His design. She petitioned city hall for five years and finally won. Before the devastating hurricanes that struck New Orleans in 2005, Kay had a full program of helping homeless women and children transition into their own homes, providing job skills, counseling, and spiritual witness as needed to assist them in being restored to a productive life. Kay discovered God's best in what it means to minister in a holistic way to people in need.

Following the hurricanes, many people were concerned about Kay and those God entrusted to her care in New Orleans. When we finally heard from her, she was back in rural Mississippi where she and her families had fled the storm. First securing a safe place for the families, she then went to her home community to ride out the storm with her parents. When I met Kay several days after the storm, she was busy doing what God had called her to do—meeting the needs of others in a holistic fashion. She and others were going from one house to another in the community to help assess the damage, clear roads, and identify those in need.

They also set up a food distribution site for those affected by the storms and managed to make cell phone contact with people outside the storm area to alert them to this pocket of folks where help had not arrived yet. They were lacking food, water, and other essential health-care items. Along with a local pastor and his wife, Kay and two of her staff arranged the fellowship hall of the church for organizing supplies. They created a system for filling food boxes and alerted the community once they knew help was coming. When I asked Kay how she was doing after all the difficulties they experienced, her response was, "I'm doing great. I'll be a better missionary after all this now that I know what it means to be homeless."

Kay's advice? "If you want to find fulfillment, purpose, meaning in life, and a peace that passes all understanding, answer God's call." Kay also understands that "the purpose of giftedness is stewardship and service, not selfishness."

Giving back

Mark 12 tells the story of an experience Jesus had with His disciples one day when He tried to teach them the real meaning of stewardship. He was observing the crowd "putting their money into the temple treasury. Many rich people threw in large amounts. But a poor widow came and put in two very small copper coins, worth only a fraction of a penny." Jesus told His disciples, "this poor widow has put more into the treasury than all the others. They all gave out of their wealth; but she, out of her poverty, put in everything" (Mark 12:41–44).

The heart of being a faithful steward is to see all of life as that which God owns. Out of His deep love for us, His creation, He gives us all that we have and all that we are, hoping that we will choose to give it back to Him as a gift, an offering of ourselves, for His purposes. When we understand the truth of Jeremiah's words, that God does indeed have a plan for our lives, a plan that gives us purpose, a future lived out in hope and joy, giving back to God what is already His will be pure joy.

Well-known writer and comedienne Erma Bombeck said it well, "When I stand before God at the end of my life I would hope that I would not have a single bit of talent left and could say, I used everything you gave me."

Think about:

1. Do you have a church in your community that is struggling?
2. How can you reach out to that church? How can your church team with that church to embrace God's plan?
3. Define stewardship.
4. What is the heart of stewardship?
5. What motivated Owen Cooper to build a fertilizer plant in India? How did his actions live up to his idea of stewardship and service?

Chapter 7

Travel with a Purpose

"I am only one, but I am one;
I cannot do everything, but I can do something.
What I can do, I ought to do.
And what I ought to do,
    by God's grace, I will do."

Anonymous[1]

During the summer prior to her senior year in college Kendra Buckles, worked as an intern in our office. Bright, articulate, and gifted with words, Kendra helped write news releases for various events coordinated by our staff. One of those was a missions project on the border between San Diego,

California, and Mexico. What started out as just a volunteer missions trip became so much more as God used this experience to continue His work in her life.

Of her experience, Kendra wrote, "Sipping on my complimentary soft drink and staring out of the airplane window, I found myself wondering: *What made this missions trip different? Why was WMU's FamilyFEST℠ in San Diego and Tijuana unlike any other missions trip I have ever taken? I have had dirtier clothes, sorer feet, and worse sunburns. I have served people in just as much need and faced challenges just as great. Why has this trip been more meaningful?*

"Often, key principles of the Christian faith cannot be grasped within the walls of churches or Sunday School rooms. The most valuable lessons of New Testament Christianity are learned far from the carpeted floors and stained glass windows of our local churches."

Kendra met the 123 volunteers from ten states who arrived for orientation. She watched as they received their assignments, some in San Diego and others who would cross the border to Tijuana. She knew she would be covering all of the work sites, including Tijuana, so she listened and absorbed as much as she could from the local leadership. She heard Fernando Martinez, pastor and director of the mission center in Tijuana, share his heart for making a difference among the poor in his community. She heard the director of missions for San Diego, Dwight Simpson, describe his community as one of the most challenging places in the US for churches to minister. But this was still just an ordinary missions trip to Kendra at this point. All that was about to change, however.

Kendra continued writing: "In 1 Corinthians 12, Paul explains the theology of the 'body of Christ.' I have read the chapter numerous times and heard countless sermons on the fundamental Christian principle. However, it was FamilyFEST, one of WMU's Volunteer Connection℠ missions opportunities, that brought the sermon home. What happened in the next four days was not a missions trip; it was the work of the body of Christ. As I visited the mission sites in both Tijuana and San Diego during the next four days, I realized how God brought so many different types of people together, uniquely combining their talents and skills to serve Him.

"In San Diego, three adults from Hawaii led a Vacation Bible School alongside a Texas family working with children living at Set Free Ministries, a transitional housing and life-skills ministry in San Diego. Two adult men from Littleton, Colorado, did electric work at First Southern Baptist Church, San Diego, while their friends and family painted and cleaned outside. Teenagers and adults from California prayerwalked in the neighborhood, preparing the way for an evangelism conference that would be coming to the neighborhood in November.

"On Tuesday and Wednesday, I crossed the border to visit the Tijuana ministry sites. A pastor and 11 fellow church members from Greenwood, Mississippi, led volunteers in Vacation Bible School for children in two areas. Baptist Nursing Fellowship℠ (BNF®) and other medical volunteers conducted three medical sites. Tijuana volunteers also painted makeshift homes and delivered rice, sugar, beans, and clean water to the residents. I was able to witness families serving Christ together as mothers and fathers delivered food beside their children, teaching them how to serve and give."

When the week was over, the volunteers gathered once again to worship and share their stories over a hot meal prepared by people from Set Free Ministries who were recovering from addiction. Each person had their own perspective about the week and how God had impacted their lives through this experience.

LuAnn Marlow, a pediatric nurse practitioner from Lawrenceville, Georgia, said, "Medical missions have always been my heart. When I saw an opportunity to do a trip with my kids, I jumped at that. I wanted to instill in them a love for missions."

Doris Bryant, a nurse who has participated in five trips with Baptist Nursing Fellowship, wanted to be involved this time so she could bring her 13-year-old granddaughter. She said, "I saw the evidence of God's hand as I watched people from many places work together as a team. Many may have come with preconceived notions, but all worked together to show the love of God to a people who have little hope."

This had been a significant answer to prayer for the team leader, Judy Murray, a nurse from Georgia, and the WMU staff leader, Kristy Carr. Judy said, "As Kristy and I were walking in Tijuana last March, I began to pray that God would bring the individuals that He had called to participate in FamilyFEST. The people in Tijuana have poor nutritional diets and live in poverty. Their homes are made of plywood, tin, with primarily dirt floors, with no indoor plumbing or electricity. The water around them is polluted, and the people have respiratory problems from inhaling smoke from the burning trash. God does such good work. We had the volunteers here with the expertise we needed. I thank God for every person on the team."

After any mission trip, the plane trip home is a time to reflect and allow God to reveal lessons from your experiences. For me, the day spent with the medical teams brought memories of other medical missions experiences that had impacted my life. I was reminded once again of how important it is to be able to speak the language of those you are serving. How grateful I was for the interpreter when she was available! Trying to help moms and children understand that vitamins are not candy and are only to be taken once a day was a bit challenging. I'm quite sure all my hand signs and feeble attempts at a few Spanish words provided some much needed laughter for those who were watching at the time! Despite the communication challenges I will not forget for some time the faces, the smiles, and the extreme poverty in which they live.

Kendra concluded her writing: "I knew that although the FamilyFEST volunteers crossed all lines of age and geography, varying in profession, experience, and talent, we all had one thing in common—God had prepared us to do a great work for Him, and it took all of us to accomplish it.

"The pilot's message broke into my thoughts of FamilyFEST, forcing me to focus on the fact the plane was about to land and the trip was officially over. However, instead of the twinges of sadness that normally pervade when a missions trip is over and the work is done, I am filled with comfort and joy. I know the body of Christ does not work together just on trips; 1 Corinthians 12:12 states, 'The body is a unit, though it is made up of many parts; and though all its parts are many, they form one body. So it is with Christ.' As every man, woman, teenager, and child returned home, I know God will continue to use us to glorify His kingdom in our own homes and communities, just as we witnessed Him do in Tijuana and San Diego."

Following the Shepherd

God uses every experience in our lives to grow us into the people He desires us to be. Times of Scripture study, prayer experiences, worship, life experiences on our jobs, in our homes, and in our neighborhoods, all provide a foundation for Him to work. Through these experiences He is actively shaping and calling us for just the right moment. He uses the simplest, most insignificant assignments as well as the most complex to provide those "aha" moments where we see Him at work and we begin to understand how He wants us to live. We are better able to embrace His call because He has made it personal for us through our own experience.

Kendra and those of us who worked alongside her during the missions experience in Mexico and San Diego brought together our everyday professional skills, unique gifts, and a desire to serve in Christ's name. When each person who volunteered heard about the needs and learned about the opportunity to work in this place, God was already working in their lives. They were sensitized to His voice and were ready to respond to His call.

John 10 reminds us that we are like sheep following a shepherd whose voice is familiar to us. Jesus said, "The man who enters by the gate is the shepherd of his sheep. The watchman opens the gate for him, and the sheep listen to his voice. He calls his own sheep by name and leads them out. When he has brought out all his own, he goes on ahead of them, and his sheep follow him because they know his voice. . . . I am the good shepherd; I know my sheep and my sheep know me" (John 10:2–4, 14).

Volunteer missions experiences provide the opportunity for us to respond to the inner pull on our hearts to serve as we grow in our understanding of what it means to be a Christ follower. As we mature in our faith, we know His voice, and we will naturally look for ways to serve because of the model Christ provided throughout His own life.

My own experiences in volunteer missions projects began as a young pastor's wife working with Acteens®. I knew very little about missions, Acteens, or WMU®, but I knew God wanted me to build relationships with the teenage girls in our first church. One of the greatest benefits of Acteens is the opportunity it provides for teenage girls to be mentored by Christian women in a setting where girls can talk about the issues they face with other girls. In addition, girls and their leaders discover ways to reach out to their community. From the very beginning of my experience as an Acteens leader, we began to study missions together and we discovered ways we could serve others in our community. We found that working together toward a common goal brought us closer together and helped us see the bigger picture of what Christ wanted from us as His followers. My commitment work with teenage girls carried on into each church where my husband served as pastor and even later as we became just members when he served as a hospital chaplain. For more than 25 years, Acteens and ministries with teenagers have played a significant role in my own spiritual growth as a follower of Christ. My life has been enriched by all the girls who have shared this love for missions with me.

Some of the greatest moments of spiritual growth among the girls and leaders occurred as we served away from home on volunteer projects. In the inner city of New Orleans, former Friendship House missionary Carolyn McClendon offered our Acteens one of the best experiences in missions. While working with the children of the French Quarter, we learned to plan and to develop meaningful activities to develop a faith foundation for these children with limited resources. We experienced how much a person can accomplish with only basic tools. Carolyn knew her children well and cared deeply for their basic life needs, but she also cared about helping young people develop spiritually. She invested her time and energy and a great deal of patience as she allowed inexperienced and often very privileged youth an opportunity to grow and develop. That same tradition continues today as the New Orleans missionaries invest themselves in not only the children and youth of their city but in the youth of our churches, realizing they can play a significant role in their faith development as well. In many other places across the US the commitment of other missionaries to help develop teenagers into our future leaders with a Christian view of the world continues, and I am most grateful for each of them.

In the midst of hard work and serious lessons in the French Quarter, there were also those moments of sheer joy and laughter. Eating beignets at midnight, talking well beyond the mandated time for lights out, getting lost in the city with their driver (namely me) making many U-turns in places I probably was not supposed to, has provided memories for all of us that will last throughout our lives. Seeing these former Acteens today and the leadership they are providing in so many different areas of service affirms the role I assumed many years ago. They have become a physician, a seminary-trained minister to students, a social worker, a Christian attorney serving in the area of domestic violence, a young woman who has traveled the world ministering to hurting women, on and on the list goes. Young women whom God is calling to serve Him vocationally and through the church found their earliest concepts of God's call through Acteens.

Volunteer missions offers many avenues for growing as Christ followers and developing a broader view of God's world. Sometimes the roadblock to responding is not knowing how to get started or where to go to accomplish the most good with our specific skills. For those reasons and more, WMU provides preplanned missions experiences for anyone who desires to serve in addition to Acteens and Youth on Mission℠ assignments. We realize that families are the best unit for service since everyone can learn together. What better way for children to learn about serving God than by watching parents or grandparents serve?

Mission trips have played a significant role in my own life, particularly at certain points of decision making. During the spring and summer of 1999, I participated in a prayer-walk in a Muslim country, provided leadership for experiences in California and Alaska, joined a Habitat for

Humanity project in Cleveland, Ohio, and rebuilt a church in the Mississippi Delta with Acteens. The final experience of the summer was a two-week medical project in Bosnia. The number of trips in one year was more than I had planned, but with each opportunity came the assurance that I was to go. Little did I know that God was preparing to deal with me about a major change in not only my life, but also that of my family. He was getting my attention, teaching me lessons that I needed to learn so I would have the foundation for making what was to be a tremendous life-altering decision. When the time came to embrace God's call to become the executive director of Woman's Missionary Union, each of these experiences came to the forefront of my mind, and each lesson learned provided just the perspective I needed, or God needed, to coax me into following His will.

Paul, the apostle, learned more about following Christ on missions trips than at any time in his life. His life was a mission trip! As we trace his missionary journeys throughout the Book of Acts, we read in chapter 11 that Barnabas mentored Paul on a missions trip. In chapter 13, they are recognized for their work later on by the church and are set apart again "for the work to which I have called them" (Acts 13:2). With a period of fasting, praying, and finally the laying on of hands, they are sent off again with the blessings of the church. In chapter 15, after a disagreement arose between Paul and Barnabas over John Mark's ability to serve with them, they parted ways, but the missionary journeys continued. Paul matured in his faith and became bold in his witness as he assumed the role of mentor, this time to Silas and later on to young Timothy.

Mission trips are vital tools in the hands of God to shape and reshape His chosen servants. Little wonder, then, because of Paul's experiences, he could pray with assurance for those who also believed in Christ whom he had come to know and love:

"I pray that you . . . may have power . . . to grasp how wide and long and high and deep is the love of Christ. . . . Now to him who is able to do immeasurably more than all we ask or imagine, according to his power that is at work within us, to him be glory in the church and in Christ Jesus throughout all generations" (Ephesians 3:17–18, 20–21).

Life-changing assignments

Corrie ten Boom wrote in her book *In My Father's House*, "God uses such seemingly insignificant ways to prepare us for the plan He has for our lives."[2] Many people today reflect back to a time when they were part of a volunteer missions experience, doing seemingly insignificant work, and remember how God used that experience to influence some future decision of a more serious nature.

On a visit to the national headquarters of Habitat for Humanity, I met a woman who appeared to me to be working full-time with the organization. She was young and enthusiastic and seemed to know a lot about the inner workings of the company. Following our tour, I felt comfortable enough to ask about her personal experience with Habitat— where was she from, and how long had she been with the organization. I was surprised to learn that she was a volunteer who accepted a short-term assignment right out of college at the corporate headquarters. She thought she would enjoy learning something new and spending a summer in the South. When her time was completed, however, she was hooked on the ministry and signed on for a second, longer volunteer assignment. She was drawing near to the close of it and was now seeking permanent employment with them. She laughed as she admitted it was not in her plans to come to Georgia, a long way away from family, and remain at a job that brought very little financial reward. Through her short-term volunteer missions commitment, God called her to this ministry.

Volunteer missions assignments can be life-changing. The time spent away from home allows us to be more focused on Him and what He has for us to learn and to do. As we respond to the needs we are confronted with, we learn something new each time about our abilities and ourselves. It is during times like these that God speaks to us, and we are better able to hear His voice. But an occasional missions trip will not build within us the strong foundation for living a missions lifestyle every day if that is the only missions influence in our daily lives. The learning curve for understanding God's worldview is much steeper than something a once-a-year trip can offer. It is a vital part but not the only part. As we embrace what it means to be a maturing follower of Christ, we will realize it takes multiple aspects of developing as a believer to shape our lives until they are complete. Regular, ongoing Scripture study, discipleship, missions education, and worship are the things that God uses in addition to the experiences in our lives, volunteer trips included.

When God speaks to us

The prophet Isaiah reveals in Scripture how God uses many ways, including life experiences, to get our attention, especially during a time of crisis. In the Book of Isaiah, we find the story of how God used a time of national crisis in his country to get the attention of Isaiah. The death of the king had thrown the entire country into turmoil. Isaiah sought solace in the one place that was constant for him, the temple. In doing what was natural for him, engaging in the act of worship, he had a profound encounter with God.

In Isaiah 6 we read: "In the year that King Uzziah died, I saw the Lord seated on a throne, high and exalted, and the train of his robe filled the temple. Above him were seraphs, each with six wings: With two wings they covered their faces, with two they covered their feet, and with two they were flying. And they were calling to one another: 'Holy, holy, holy is the Lord Almighty; the whole earth is full of his glory.' At the sound of their voices the doorposts and thresholds shook and the temple was filled with smoke. 'Woe to me!' I cried. 'I am ruined! For I am a man of unclean lips, and I live among a people of unclean lips, and my eyes have seen the King, the Lord Almighty'" (Isaiah 6:1–5).

After the seraph touched his lips with a live coal from the fire, Isaiah heard the voice of God saying, "'See, this has touched your lips; your guilt is taken away and your sin atoned for.' Then I heard the voice of the Lord saying, 'Whom shall I send? And who will go for us?'" (Isaiah 6:8).

In the experience of worship, Isaiah saw the Lord for who He is in all His power and majesty. He saw a loving, forgiving God who wanted to reveal His purpose for Isaiah's life. Then he saw himself for who he really was—a sinner, unclean and living among an unclean nation. Hearing God's voice and understanding His call to follow Him, Isaiah realized he could do no less than offer all of His life to God. His words of commitment, "Here am I. Send me!" (v. 8) remind us that we, too, are basically unclean, but with God's call comes His cleansing and His power to respond.

Embracing God's mission takes place through the common, everyday experiences of our lives and the special times set aside to focus on God. This includes the regular practice of worship. Often we attend a worship service and leave without ever having worshipped. Worship only takes place when we have an encounter with God, when we see Him for who He is and how He wants to impact our lives. Worship is more than giving lip service to the hymns and allowing our minds to wander as the minister speaks. Worship occurs when we give the honor and reverence to God that He deserves, when we seek His face and ask for forgiveness for the times we failed to follow Him. Worship is quietly, patiently listening for God to speak, and when He does, we respond.

When a crisis comes, what has been our habit becomes the natural way we respond. If we understand and experience true worship, then we will want to seek God in a place of worship that is familiar. When worship is a regular part of who we are, God speaks to us, and our hearts and ears are tuned to hear Him.

Life-changing trip

In an earlier chapter I described a volunteer missions experience I had in Brazil. Planning for that trip was time consuming, but it was the kind of missions experience I had always wanted to be a part of. It was a large medical group with three doctors, a pharmacist, two dentists, an eye doctor; several support staff and a group whose primary task was to work with church evangelism activities and children. I had been on many different kinds of trips, but this was a nurse's dream. I could focus entirely on the medical aspects of the assignments, knowing someone else was covering the other areas well. Just days before I was to leave, I received a call from my state WMU office. I was living in Georgia at the time, and the chair of the nominating committee wanted permission to submit my name as their state WMU president. I was shocked to say the least, and my first inclination was to say no. Our daughter was leaving for college, I was working more at the hospital in a new role that I enjoyed very much, and our son was entering his freshman year of high school. I knew what she was asking, and it was a really big volunteer job.

When I hung up the phone, I remember thinking to myself, *Why didn't I just say no? Why did I promise I would think about it and pray about it while I was away?* I think at the moment I had so much on my mind about the trip, my work, and my family, I just wanted off the phone. At the same time I didn't want to hurt her feelings by refusing to even consider what the committee asked. It was an honor to be nominated; and as inadequate as I felt for the job, the least I could do was give it some thought and prayer.

I must confess there was little time on the missions trip to think about anything but the demands of the hundreds of patients waiting for us each morning when we arrived at the school to begin clinic. I was totally focused on my role and was thrilled to have the chance to see and learn about many diseases I had only read about in textbooks. The doctors were wonderful to work with, and I loved being a part of the worship services each evening even though I understood little that was said. Singing hymns in our separate languages reminded me that when God listened, He heard our words as one language.

When the clinics were finished and we packed up to return home, we spent one night in Manaus on the return flight. We had some time to reflect on all that we had experienced. We took a boat ride down the Amazon and saw villages along the shoreline with many more people in need of proper medical care. At the same time, we were overwhelmed with the natural beauty of God's creation in Brazil. The rain forest and the mighty Amazon River were breathtaking. During these moments God reminded me of how blessed I was to live in a place where medical care was so good and readily available. I had a wonderful family who supported my commitment to missions and made my being away for trips like this one possible. There was a course correction taking place within my heart and my attitude about how I was to serve in the coming days.

Several weeks after returning home I called the chair of the nominating committee and told her I would accept the committee's nomination, and if it were God's will for me to lead Georgia WMU, He would guide those who voted in the spring. I had such a sense of God's direction and timing with this invitation to serve and the commitment I had already made to go to Brazil. God speaks to us in worship inside a church or in worship on the Amazon River, or on a volunteer mission trip. When He speaks, if we are listening, we will know His voice and will answer as Isaiah did, "Here am I. Send me."

Think about:

1. In what daily experiences can God grow us into His people?
2. In what ways are mission trips valuable?
3. What can motivate an individual to make life-changing decisions?
4. Why is it important for families to work together on missions projects?
5. What are some of the roadblocks that are keeping you from working on missions projects? How can you remove those roadblocks?

CHAPTER 8

ACT ON WHAT YOU KNOW

"The life of faith is not a life of mounting up with wings but a life of walking and not fainting. . . . Faith never knows where it is being led, but it loves and knows the One who is leading."

Oswald Chambers[1]

In 1979, after two years of preparation and seeking God's direction, my husband and I were appointed as career missionaries. In our interviews our one request of the mission sending board was that we both be appointed, my husband as a church planter/pastor and me as a registered nurse in medical missions. We each individually experienced God's call to missions at different times in our lives, and it had been reaffirmed as His call for us as a family. We followed all the procedures that led us to believe that at the end of our interviews, we would have some idea of possible places of service for our particular calling. The weekend came and went and we returned home without any sense of direction regarding the place where God was calling us to serve.

As weeks went by, we waited patiently, praying for a clear sign of where we were to serve. Late one evening, the phone rang and a man introduced himself and apologized for not meeting us weeks before during our interviews. He explained that when my husband and I interviewed, he was out of the country at a meeting of missionaries in the Caribbean where he discovered their number one request in the area of personnel. On one particular island, a missionary family was returning home on a medical emergency. The man was a church planter/pastor, and someone was needed immediately to take over his work. The caller then said the missionaries mentioned that if the replacement's spouse happened to be a nurse, it would be perfect, since their next great need was for a second nurse to help implement a community health program. The caller said that all the way home he kept thinking, *Where on earth am I going to find a couple that meets this specific description that is ready to come to the field immediately?* Upon returning to his office, he found our file on his desk and the question: Do you have requests for a couple with these specific skills?

I knew instantly God was sending the clearest, most unmistakable sign of His call about our possible appointment. When the caller named the country, we told him we had never heard of it, but we were sure it was where God was leading us. The first thing we did after hanging up the phone was find an encyclopedia to learn something about St. Vincent!

In the weeks that followed, some of our family and friends who did not quite understand our sense of call asked some very practical questions, such as: You're taking the children where? What kind of house will you live in? What will you do for transportation? What are the possibilities of schools for the children? Even, how much money are you going to be paid? My husband and I have laughed many times about how absolutely absurd it must have seemed to people when we could not answer these basic questions. As hard as we tried to tell them what we were going to do and why, they continued to have that puzzled look on their faces. We understood their obvious confusion when all we could say was, "Yes, we've been hired to do a certain job in a country we've never visited, where we don't know anything about the living conditions, education, or health care, and, no, we forgot to ask how much they were going to pay us." How ridiculous it must have seemed on a logical level to accept a job under those circumstances.

But this wasn't just any job. We were in the midst of watching God perform a miracle in our lives by moving us beyond what seemed logical to what was a deeply spiritual experience. In Isaiah, we are reminded that God's ways are not our ways. He said, "For my thoughts are not your thoughts, neither are your ways my ways. As the heavens are higher than the earth so are my ways higher than your ways" (Isaiah 55:8–9). Sometimes God's way of communicating His plan is not in a logical manner from a human point of view. Embracing God's call in our lives may not seem to be the most logical decision at times. It may appear that all the details are not worked out, that the specifics are too vague. We are always to pray and seek God's direction until we are certain He is leading. But there will be times when He calls us without giving us all the answers.

The writer of Hebrews reminds us, "By faith, Abraham, when called to go to a place he would later receive as an inheritance, obeyed and went, even though he did not know where he was going. . . . By faith, he made his home in the promised land like a stranger in a foreign country. . . . By faith, Abraham, even though he was past age—and Sarah herself was barren—was enabled to become a father because he considered him faithful who had made the promise" (Hebrews 11:8, 9, 11).

Part of the journey of following Christ is learning to exercise trust, depending on God to provide all that is needed for a certain task. Because we are so often inclined to take the credit ourselves, it may be the only way people will see God at work instead of us. Paul explained it to the Corinthians by saying, "We live by faith, not by sight" (2 Corinthians 5:76).

Following His leading

History reveals many people who have embraced God's call when they had only a glimpse of what it might mean. One of those was William Carey, a poor shoemaker in England, who dared to speak a new thought about the responsibility of Christians to share the gospel with those he perceived to be in "heathen nations." Long before world travel was common-place, he became fascinated with the maps of the world and kept one over his cobbler's bench as he prayed for the world.

One day he openly shared his thoughts, which were promptly greeted with a rebuke: "Young man, sit down. When God pleases to convert the heathen, He will do it without your aid or mine."[2] Despite those who chastised him for his outrageous beliefs, Carey continued to heed God's call to speak on behalf of those who had never heard.

By 1792, the pull of God's call towards missions became so strong he could do no less than commit to go to India even though he lacked firsthand knowledge of the country and its people. He went without knowing how difficult life would become in this foreign land. Because of the faithful-ness of God and the certainty of His call, Carey was able to remain faithful for 41 years in his service. His life became a testimony to the people of India as he shared with them the story of God's unchanging power to change lives.

William Carey's life and writings changed the face of the modern missionary movement. His famous words of chal-lenge to the people of his day continue to inspire many today: "Expect great things [from God]; attempt great things [for God]."[3]

There are other great figures from history who heard God's call and, without having a clear path laid out before them, followed His leading. Florence Nightingale went against the culture of her day to move from a woman of means and social standing to the lowest of low professions, a nurse. Her quest for answers to the reasons behind the spread of disease and her attention to details in the care of her patients changed the face of nursing care during the Crimean War. Her courage in the midst of an unknown enemy called infection has been a symbol of strength for many entering the highly respected profession today. She couldn't possibly have known where her decision to follow God's call would lead, but she served with the assurance of His presence and a commitment to be a part of His plan for her life. Today Florence Nightingale is an example for all nurses who have heard God's call and commit their lives to serving the needs of others through quality health care.

We will seldom have all the answers to our questions when we make our decisions. Like William Carey and Florence Nightingale, we have to act based on what we know at any given time, sensing that God is in control and will lead us each step of the way as we seek His direction.

Continuing education

Becoming a lifelong learner is essential for the growing Christian, especially as we learn to make decisions with only partial knowledge at times about any given situation. Many people today constantly seek ways to improve themselves through higher education or cross training in their professions. We acknowledge that learning is a process that is never complete. Professional organizations for accountants, nurses, lawyers, doctors, and numerous others mandate yearly updates through required numbers of hours spent in seminars or conferences. It is assumed that learning is a continuous process that requires attention and structure.

What would happen if we carried this same idea over to our personal growth as Christians? How we respond to God's call in our lives might be greatly impacted if we intentionally sought continuous learning experiences—experiences to help us grow in our knowledge of God's Word, His world, and His design for our lives.

Dellanna O'Brien, in her book *Timeless Virtues*, wrote that lifelong learners need three things: an insatiable curiosity, an open mind, and to be intentional about learning.[4] Curiosity about the things around us, the people we meet, the world far from our doorstep will keep us learning long after we complete our formal education. A basic curiosity about life prompts us to ask questions, to research a topic we know little about, or simply read a good book on the subject. Without a healthy curiosity we become complacent about learning.

An open mind means we are willing to consider an alternative point of view. Our way may not always be the only way. We can discuss openly a new thought without immediately negating the possibility. We recognize that we might not have all the answers, that our concept or information might not be the complete answer. We're open to change if a new view with facts is presented. Learning can only take place when our minds are open to the thoughts and opinions of others when presented with sensible data.

Learning may happen even when we don't plan for it; but to be sure learning takes place, we need to be intentional about it. We sign up for a class at the local college or a seminar through our church or school system. We join the local library and participate in its educational opportunities. We should never be satisfied with our current level of knowledge, but seek to grow intellectually at every opportunity. We need to take seriously God's command to love Him with our mind and offer only the best mind possible back to Him.

We can be lifelong learners who build a foundation with which to make decisions on a moment's notice. Proverbs 10:14 says, "Wise men store up knowledge." We can learn to take action without having all the answers if we have cultivated these things as a normal part of our lives.

Dellanna reminds us that there are some things we can and should do that will help us discern God's will when we sense His leading. Begin by praying for understanding and discerning God's direction; reflect on those things we have learned previously from Scripture and other life lessons; be open to the new lesson God may have for us when we least expect it; listen to the voice of the Holy Sprit; be open to change how we think or act as God leads us; and finally, act on whatever knowledge you have at the time to make the decision. She says that "an increased knowledge of God's world and its peoples gives us a deeper understanding of the measure of His love for us all."[5] What better reason do we need to keep on learning?

There will come a time in every decision-making situation when we simply must act. A sense of "rightness" wells up within us and we realize we must move forward. This is where faith becomes the foundation for our actions. Looking back after prayerfully stepping out in faith to make a decision allows us to have the assurance that God was indeed with us, stirring us to a response. Then we know what the writer of Hebrews meant when he said, "Now faith is being sure of

what we hope for and certain of what we do not see"
(Hebrews 11:1).

Rightness

I have heard many people talk about a sense of rightness
when they respond to God's call. It has been true in my own
life, but it has helped me to understand it better when I hear
others share this truth in their lives as well. Travis Collins is
a good friend and the pastor of Bon Air Baptist Church, a
large church in Richmond, Virginia. He served as a missionary journeyman for two years, a career missionary in Nigeria,
and in other places as a pastor. When asked to describe his
call to service, Travis affirmed God's gift of a sense of rightness in his life at critical times.

"God's call in my life unfolded. As a 16-year-old working
for the summer at a Christian camp, I sensed that I had been
cut out for what we then called full-time Christian service.
Because I loved to sing, I felt like God must want me to be a
music minister. I enrolled in Samford University, and, on the
first day of my second semester of music theory, Professor
Bob Burroughs said something like, 'My job is to weed out
those of you who really aren't supposed to be here.' And it
worked on me. I realized during that semester that music was
not my calling.

"I chose psychology as a major, sensing that I would end
up in some kind of people business. I applied to go on a missions trip to NYC, and Dr. Bill Cowley read my application
for the trip. He befriended me and became a significant
influencer in my life. I still remember descending the stairs
from the cafeteria and having Dr. Cowley say, 'Aren't you

Travis Collins?' From that moment, God used Dr. Cowley to set my life on its ultimate course. Soon Dr. Cowley asked me if I'd considered service as a missionary journeyman. I decided to consider it, frankly, because I didn't have any real prospects for postcollege life. I was appointed for service in Venezuela.

"The memory of my call to career international missionary service is still clear. I was walking across the street in Caracas, Venezuela, after a worship service. I had this deep sense of rightness about what I was doing. I had this deep feeling that I was born for international missions. I loved the adventure of speaking another language and living in another culture. But there was more—there was that deep sense that God was smiling on my overseas service."

Travis began seeking what vocational approach God wanted him to use in mission service. He preached his first sermon while serving in Maracaibo because a friend, recognizing he was in a time of seeking, asked him to. When he finished, he said he felt the same sense of rightness that he had felt earlier when he knew God had called him to career missions. He returned home after his two-year assignment, married a girl from college who had told him on their first date that she was called to be a missionary. They went to seminary, and in 1991, following completion of Travis's PhD work, moved to Nigeria where he taught at the Nigerian Baptist Theological Seminary.

But God's call takes twists and turns that we do not always count on. As with many missionaries, the concern for parents and children was never far away. Travis's father suffered a stroke, and it was necessary for the couple to return home to care for him. Since that time, God has called Travis to serve in pastoral roles in a variety of places. He continued to experience God's call and a sense of rightness with each new avenue of service.

Travis says, "Each time I have sensed God's new call it has come in what I refer to as a deep sense of rightness. No email from heaven, but a profound impression in my spirit that my Father and Creator is pleased with this. Living out God's call has its challenges. My calling to the leadership of a fairly large church often brings some loneliness, the weight of momentous decisions, and periods of discouragement. Yet I still have that same deep sense of rightness that I had back when I was crossing the street in Caracas—that God is pleased with my being in this role."

Travis acted on what he knew to be God's direction with each call without having all the facts and knowledge about each step. What guided him was a reoccurring sense of rightness as he sought and waited for God's direction.

Changing direction

That same sense of rightness led Grace to resign from her position at a prominent school in her city after 29 years of teaching. Her school was known for academic excellence with students who achieved the highest scores on college preentrance exams. Many students received some of the highest scholarships to college provided to graduating seniors. Grace was a part of the best education the teaching profession had to offer. At one point in her career, she began to offer help to at-risk students in a neighborhood that could only be described in terms of poverty, illiteracy, neglected children, and a high crime rate. At first she worked a few hours a month in an afterschool and summer enrichment program. But before long, she began to struggle with a sense that God was calling her to devote all of her time to help these disadvantaged students.

Hearing her tell of her journey, you sense her initial struggle with what seemed to be an impossible call. But a sense of rightness emerged and she knew God was leading her into a new, exciting, and rewarding life in the inner city. Today, Grace is a part of a ministry that helps at-risk students stay in school while also hearing about a God who has a plan for their lives. She walked away from a good salary and a prestigious position because she sensed it was the right thing to do according to God's design.

That same sense of rightness was clear when Larry and I accepted God's call to serve as missionaries in St. Vincent in 1979. We did the best we could to answer the questions of those who struggled with our call and we moved forward with the information we had at the time. It was the adventure of a lifetime. We discovered God had gone before us and prepared the way for us to have a place to live, a way for our daughter to have an education, and a wonderful group of Christian friends to help us learn how to live in a new culture. Our understanding of God and His ways grew during our time of service. We learned to depend more on Him than on ourselves as we witnessed His provision for all that we needed. He gave us the opportunity to broaden our view of His world by trusting Him and stepping out into the unknown. I'm so glad we said yes to His call. I wouldn't have missed it for anything.

"My son, do not forget my teaching, but keep my
   commands in your heart,
for they will prolong your life many years and
   bring you prosperity.
Let love and faithfulness never leave you;
bind them around your neck, write them on the
   tablet of your heart.
Then you will win favor and a good name in the
   sight of God and man.
Trust in the Lord with all your heart and lean not
   on your own understanding;
in all your ways acknowledge him, and he will
   make your paths straight."

Proverbs 3:1–6

Think about:

1. What does being a lifelong learner mean?
2. What are some continuing education projects you have done for your career?
3. What are some continuing education projects you have done for the Lord?
4. What does rightness mean?
5. When have you experienced a feeling of rightness?

Section 3

Live the Mission
of God

If you cannot cross the ocean,
And the distant lands explore,
You can find the lost around you,
You can help them at your door;
If you cannot give your thousands,
You can give the widow's mite;
What you truly give for Jesus
Will be precious in His sight.

Let none hear you idly saying,
"There is nothing I can do,"
While the lost of earth are dying,
And the Master calls for you;
Take the task He gives you gladly;
Let His work your pleasure be;

Answer quickly when He calls you,
"Here am I, send me, send me."
The Baptist Hymnal (1991 edition)

What does it mean to really live the call? I think these words written by Daniel March explain it well. God is looking for people who will "walk worthy of the Lord, fully pleasing him" (Colossians 1:10 NKJV). Following God's call may not be easy, but we follow because of His great love and sacrifice willingly given on the Cross. Once we hear His call and grasp the depth of peace and joy we find in following His call, the call then becomes the driving force behind all that we do.

Calling comes decisively and clearly when we are listening for God's voice. He desires that we follow His call with a deep sense of commitment and devotion wherever it may lead. We will then be able to respond with the words of the hymn writer, "Here am I, send me." The truth is there is no other way to find what makes life really worth it but to live the call.

Live the Call

CHAPTER 9

WALK WORTHY

"Walk worthy of the Lord, fully pleasing Him, being fruitful in every good work and increasing in the knowledge of God."

Colossians 1:10 NKJV

In the 1920s, WMU helped established a training school in Bucharest, Romania, where women and missionaries could learn missions principles and techniques for sharing their faith. A woman named Lidia received training at the school, and following graduation, went to Moldova to teach and train women in missions as she was taught. She led the women of Moldova to establish a women's missions organization. She visited in their villages and prisons, teaching them how to follow Christ.

Communism came to Moldova. In 1941 Lidia was severely beaten, mistreated, and sentenced to 25 years in prison because she was a Christian. She was released after 15 years and returned to Moldova to begin again to train the women as she had before. Years later, when communism was no longer a threat and Lidia was old, she called for a young woman named Olga. She said she wanted to teach Olga everything she knew, what she learned at the training school years before. She wanted to teach her to do kingdom work. So Olga learned, and it was as if Lidia was passing on the mantle of faith and responsibility for the gospel among the women of Moldova, which Olga accepted as a call from God.

Since that time, Olga has carried on the work started by Lidia. She faithfully follows God's call and models her service after the one who influenced her life in so many ways. In the foyer of First Baptist Church of Kishinev, I'm told, there is a picture of Lidia; a tribute to the one who served as Olga's mentor and friend so long ago. Inscribed on the picture are these words: "Lidia, our most faithful daughter of our most faithful God."

Colossian Christians

Colossians 1:10 (NKJV) commands that as believers we are to "walk worthy of the Lord, fully pleasing Him." Lidia knew what it meant to "walk worthy." Her entire life was lived in an effort to "fully please Him." Because she walked worthy, Olga learned to do so as well. Today in Moldova many women are learning what it means to hear God's call and what faithfulness to follow His call looks like.

There are so many demands for our time and attention, so many messages hurled at us through advertising, media, and movies. In a culture that cries out for us to be number one, to seek material success at all costs, the call of God to walk worthy can fall on deaf ears. Scripture tells us that we are not the only generation to face such contradictory messages. This problem has existed since the very beginning of the early church. What can we learn from their response to this dilemma? How can we remain focused on living the call of God in the midst of mixed messages? Paul gives us some advice in his letter to the Colossian Christians who were faced with a similar situation.

First of all, who were the Colossians? The city of Colossae was located in western Asia Minor, approximately 100 miles east of Ephesus. It was one of those cities where a rich mixture of traders and travelers passed through, contributing to its growing wealth. It became a textile center partly due to its prime location on the River Lycus. The richness of the soil created wonderful grazing land, leading to an abundance of sheep. As a result, this encouraged a strong wool industry; and coupled with the presence of chalk in the riverbed, a dye industry flourished as well. The city became a cosmopolitan mixture of Jews and Gentiles from all across Asia Minor, which provided a colorful culture that also fostered a climate of varying religious beliefs. It was because of this infusion of various religious beliefs and practices that mixed messages began to surface and influence the early church. After hearing about this, Paul felt a need to write the Colossian Christians a letter.

Paul, to our knowledge, never visited Colossae. He knew

about the church at Colossae from Epaphras, someone he describes in the first chapter of his letter to the Colossians as "our good friend" and "a faithful worker for you" (Colossians 1: 7 CEV). Epaphras lived in Colossae, and possibly was the pastor of the church at some point. When he and Paul ended up in jail together, as mentioned in Philemon 23, Epaphras told Paul all about the church. He described their wonderful attributes as followers of Christ but also raised a concern about the influence of other religious teachings on the church. This kind of influence on the early churches was not new to Paul. He was well aware of how outside philosophies and teachings that were not in line with the teachings of Christ could corrupt a new young church. He wrote many warnings to various churches about avoiding false teachers and doctrine as noted throughout the New Testament.

What did Paul hope to accomplish with his letter? At the outset, he wanted to be a source of encouragement and affirmation for their strong foundation of faith received in their beginnings. Secondly, he wanted to strengthen their belief in Christ. He reminded them that what they knew from the beginning was the correct doctrine and not what they were being exposed to at this time. Paul's message was simple— Christ is sufficient for all of the Christian life. They didn't need to look for anything more to add to the message they heard in the beginning from Epaphras. His letter provides a beautiful model for us as followers of Christ today of ways that we can affirm new Christians in what is good and tenderly move them away from teachings that might harm their faith. And finally, in the first chapter, he provides a model for how to pray for others to remain strong in their Christian walk.

"Each time we pray for you, we thank God, the Father of our Lord Jesus Christ. We have heard of your faith in Christ and of your love for all of God's people, because what you hope for is kept safe for you in heaven. You first heard about this hope when you believed the true message, which is the good news. The good news is spreading all over the world with great success. It has spread in that same way among you, ever since the first day you learned the truth about God's wonderful kindness from our good friend Epaphras. He works together with us for Christ and is a faithful worker for you. He is also the one who told us about the love that God's Spirit has given you" (Colossians 1:3–8 CEV).

Paul's letter to the Colossian Christians is consistent with many of his other letters. He begins with a greeting as seen in verses 1 and 2, identifying himself and to whom the letter is written. He then begins to write a prayer, which is often his custom as well. He thanked God for the good things seen in the church—their faith in Christ and their love expressed for all people. He acknowledged evidence of their hope for things to come. In essence, Paul said these are the things you learned from the beginning, and they were correct; don't forsake them or lose them.

He goes on to identify three elements essential for living the Christian faith—faith, love, and hope. This is not the first time Paul clustered these three fruits or evidences of the presence of the Holy Spirit at work in the life of a believer. The most familiar passage is found in 1 Corinthians 13:13, but they appear in a different order. "Now these three remain: faith, hope and love. But the greatest of these is love." These core elements are also found in 1 Thessalonians 1:3 and 5:8;

Hebrews 6:10–12 and 10:22–24; Galatians 5:5–6; and Ephesians 4:2–5. Paul consistently recognized that without the presence of these three core elements, one could doubt the professed belief in Christ.

William Barclay, in his commentary on Colossians wrote: "The Christian life must show loyalty to Christ and love to men. The Christian must have faith; he must know what he believes. But he must also have love for men; he must turn belief into action. . . . The Christian faith is not only a conviction of the mind; it is also an overflow of the heart. It is not only correct thought; it is loving conduct. Faith in Christ and love to men are the twin pillars of the Christian life. That faith and that love depend on the hope that is laid up in heaven." He quotes C. F. D. Moule who adds, "The hope is the certainty that in spite of the world's ways and the world's standards God's way of love has the last word."[1]

Paul affirmed the outward evidence of the Spirit's work as seen in their lives by the way they loved others. He said it was an expression of their faith and hope in God. He offered thanksgiving in his prayer for them and then entered into a time of intercession on their behalf.

"We have not stopped praying for you since the first day we heard about you. In fact, we always pray that God will show you everything he wants you to do and that you may have all the wisdom and understanding that his Spirit gives. Then you will live a life that honors the Lord, and you will always please him by doing good deeds. You will come to know God even better. His glorious power will make you patient and strong enough to endure anything and you will be truly happy. I pray that you will be grateful to God for letting you have part in what he has promised his people in the kingdom of light" (Colossians 1:9–12 CEV).

What a beautiful prayer on behalf of people he had never met but loved because of their love for Christ! Paul's prayer of intercession encompasses several requests. First of all, he asked that they might know God's will. The NKJV says, "that you may be filled with the knowledge of His will in all wisdom and spiritual understanding." Sometimes we lose sight of the ultimate purpose of prayer, which should be for us to discover God's will for our lives, not our trying to convince Him that our will is best. The prayer Jesus modeled includes the words, "Thy will be done in earth as it is in heaven," indicating that our prayers should be focused on God's will, not ours (Matthew 6:10 KJV). Paul is asking that the Christians in Colossae truly understand the great truths of the gospel and that they will be able to apply those truths to their everyday lives. A knowledge of God's will leads to a growing intimacy with God's character; as our understanding of His character grows we will be better able to become more like His Son.

Malcolm Tolbert, in the *Layman's Bible Book Commentary* explains, "Too often we think of the will of God as a plan traced out for the individual life. We think of it in terms of career choices, marriage, changing jobs, and so forth. . . . The will of God in the broadest sense is his plan to redeem his people. In a narrower sense it has to do with the way we fit into that plan as individuals. In order to know God's will we need the Spirit's gift of wisdom and understanding."[2]

Shouldn't this be our heart's desire, to be filled with the knowledge of God's will so that we can know without a doubt our part in His plan for redeeming His people; and then to have the wisdom and understanding of how to apply it to our lives each day? Wisdom gives us spiritual insights that aid our understanding of how to apply these truths to our lives.

One day I was visiting with a leader of a large organization, as we shared concerns that we both had about leadership. He asked if he could pray for me, and if so, what would I like for him to pray for specifically. I was humbled by his request and simply asked him to pray that I might have wisdom when facing times of decision making. He paused for a moment and then asked if he could expand that prayer on my behalf. He said he learned that all the wisdom in the world would not help him unless he had the courage to act on it once he received it. Since that day I have altered my prayer as well. I ask God for His wisdom, but I also ask Him to give me the courage to act when the time is right.

Paul's prayer doesn't stop with his request for wisdom and understanding. He goes on to reveal the outcome of a life that is infused with wisdom and an understanding of how to live within God's will. Paul says, "Then you will live a life that honors the Lord" (Colossians 1:10 CEV). Other translations say it this way: "That you may walk worthy of the Lord, fully pleasing Him" (NKJV), and "you may live a life worthy of the Lord and may please Him in every way" (NIV).

The Greek word used in the original text means "to walk" or "to lead a life." The metaphor about life being a walk is seen often in Scripture, especially in Paul's writings. He referred to it more than 30 times. Harold Songer wrote in his book *Colossians: Christ Above All*, "The understanding of

Christian life involved in this expression needs to be emphasized. Walking involves both direction and progress. A Christian is a person on the move. Being Christian is more than having achieved a certain set of moral habits; being Christian means to be on one's way to a goal. A Christian should be developing into what Jesus Christ would have him [or her] be."[3]

The meaning behind the phrase to "walk worthy" is fleshed out in the remaining verses of Paul's prayer. If we are walking worthy of the Lord, Paul says we will do "good deeds" and we will "come to know God even better"; we will be "patient and strong enough to endure anything" and we will be "truly happy" (Colossians 1:10–11 CEV). When we understand God's mission in the world and His plan for our lives as a part of His mission, when we have embraced His unique call for ourselves as our own, we will begin to "walk worthy," living a life that demonstrates steady growth in these attributes. We will recognize that the strength found to "walk worthy" in good times is easy; but when difficulties come, we will need all of the power God will grant us to stay strong. To run a race with endurance and patience means we can see the finish line despite the roadblocks that may come our way. We can patiently work our way through them for the sake of the call that we are following because of the One who gives us the power and the strength for each day.

Finally, as Paul continued his prayer, he made three requests of God for the Colossian believers. He asked that they become "grateful" because of God's call, that He has allowed them to have a part in His great work of bringing people out of darkness and into His wonderful light of salvation. He reminded them in Colossians 1:13–14, "God rescued us from the dark power of Satan and brought us into the kingdom of his dear Son who forgives our sins and sets us free" (CEV). *The Message* says it this way: "God rescued us from dead-end alleys and dark dungeons. He's set us up in the kingdom of the Son he loves so much, the Son who got us out of the pit we were in, got rid of the sins we were doomed to keep repeating" (Colossians 1:13–14 *The Message*).

Why is gratitude so important? Living a life of gratitude signals we are attuned with the One who has called us and provides the strength to live within that call every day. When we are grateful, we recognize we do not have the power within our own strength to live worthy lives. We also cannot follow God out of fear or to win some favor. Living a life of gratitude signals an awareness on our part that all God has and is doing for us is because He loves us and gave the best he could give to bring us to Himself—His Son, Jesus. What a wonderful gift of grace! The only possible response to such grace is gratitude.

Lidia, despite all the difficulties in her life, the persecution for her faith, and the loss of 15 years of her life and service, never forgot how to be grateful for God's gift of grace. In fact, I suspect grace is what sustained her during her years in prison. Otherwise, she would never have returned to the women of Moldova proclaiming the goodness of God and their responsibility to heed His call in service of others.

Os Guinness, in *The Call*, affirms for us that "calling is a reminder for followers of Christ that nothing in life should be taken for granted; everything in life must be received with gratitude."[4]

With hearts full of gratitude for God and His Son, we are challenged then to "Walk worthy of the Lord, fully pleasing Him, being fruitful in every good work and increasing in the knowledge of God" as we live the call.

Think about:

1. How have other religions influenced you? How do these religions influence your church?
2. Why did Paul write to the people of Colossae?
3. Why is gratitude so important?
4. What would it mean to you and your church to receive a letter from another Christian that said they were praying for you and your walk with God?
5. How can you and your church encourage other Christians to walk worthy?

CHAPTER 10

COMBINE MINISTRY AND MISSIONS

"I don't know what your destiny will be, but one thing I do know: the only ones among you who will be really happy are those who have sought and found how to serve."

Albert Schweitzer[1]

While growing up, I thought the only people God really talked to were preachers and missionaries . . . that is until He spoke to me one day. Then I began to understand He really does speak to all of His followers, and He invites us to become an avenue for others to come to know Him.

As a minister's wife and leader of a Christian nonprofit organization, I must confess that many in my circle of friends today serve in what we refer to as "professional ministry." The belief I had as a child is a very common myth found in our culture today. Many people believe that God's call is only for people going into "full-time Christian service." That phrase is usually interpreted to mean preachers, ministers on church staffs, missionaries, chaplains, and denominational workers. Nothing could be further from the truth. God speaks to all of His children who are listening, and He calls them to follow His plan for their lives, regardless of their chosen profession.

God's call is always first to Himself. We all begin at the same point—with a call to faith. The truth of the gospel for all people can be summed up in one passage of Scripture: "For God so loved the world that he gave his one and only Son, that whoever believes in him shall not perish but have eternal life" (John 3:16). Jesus goes on to remind us, "You did not choose me, but I chose you and appointed you to go and bear fruit—fruit that will last" (John 15:16). Once we understand God has chosen us to be His, and we ask Jesus to forgive us for our failures, to come and live in us and be our Lord, then God calls us to be a part of His work in the world. He calls us to "walk worthy" in our speech and in our actions because of the potential for influence we have on others. Those who know we are Christ followers are watching and listening to us, and they begin to develop receptive or closed minds, based on what they see and hear. Jesus calls us to bear fruit. The kind of fruit we bear will be a direct reflection of the relationship we have with the One we are following. In the Book of James we are reminded, "As the body without the spirit is dead, so faith without deeds is dead" (James 2:26).

Bearing fruit

In 1999 WMU committed to partner with Habitat for Humanity to build seven houses across America. Those of us who served—WMU Executive Board members along with the state and national staff—were challenged to choose at least one site and volunteer our services. I, serving as president for the organization, chose to participate in the project in Cleveland, Ohio. This project was in the inner city among row houses, necessitating the house be built narrow with two stories. Because it was the middle of the summer, we had two building shifts—one in the morning and one in the afternoon. When we weren't building, we served the community through various ministry opportunities. Some volunteers served the homeless a meal, some assisted the churches with various needs in their communities, and some of us who were nurses conducted health classes at a local, predominately Hispanic child-care center. All of the ministries were important and provided a break in the day from the hot, manual labor of construction.

I was excited about building a two-story house. I had previously participated in other Habitat projects but always a one-story house. One afternoon as we were working on the second floor I noticed that people in the apartment building next to where we were building were watching us. As the second floor went up, we were almost within touching distance of the walls of each other's building. Sometimes we heard music; sometimes we heard arguments . . . sounds that always reminded us of our close proximity to each other. Our volunteers were great. We had fun building, laughing, sharing stories, critiquing each others' lack of building expertise, and taking care of each others' wounds when we hammered the wrong way. We were a diverse group of people! One day I worked alongside a retired builder, an intensive care nurse, and a secretary. We came from different backgrounds and had different skills, but we were all believers who followed God's leadership to this place.

On the last day of our weeklong missions project, a woman came out of the building next door and asked to speak with me. For a moment I wondered if we had been making too much noise or had somehow caused a problem. My concern was immediately put to rest as she began to ask me several questions about the group. Did we know each other before we came? *No.* Were we professional builders? *Absolutely not!* Where had we come from? *A host of different states.* Did we know the woman we were building the house for? *No, but we just met her that day.* And then the last of her questions: Were we there because we were Christians? When I responded, *yes, we were,* she said she lived on the second floor of the building adjacent to where we were working. Because she did not have air-conditioning, her windows were open and she could hear what was going on as we worked. She watched us all week and noticed that even though we worked hard and the days were hot, we never said unkind words to each other. She noticed that we laughed and seemed to enjoy what we were doing. She watched us pray in the morning before beginning work. She wanted to know what made us different from other workers she had observed. She asked if I could tell her how to have what we seemed to have. She said something about Christianity and wondered if I knew someone who lived in the community who might be able to help her understand the Bible. Wow! With joy I told her about the One who had called us to her city to work. I introduced her to our local partner who promised to teach her the Bible and connect her with other believers so she could grow as a Christian.

This woman saw enough of Christ in how we conducted our lives on that project to venture out of her home for a conversation. Our actions, the way we conducted ourselves, and the fact that we traveled from our homes to come to her neighborhood to help someone we didn't know, earned us the right to share Christ in her way of thinking. She was ready and willing to hear our words that led her to know the reason behind our actions. What a disservice we would have done to her if our words and our actions had not pointed her to Christ and the power of His Word that would move her from seeking to accepting. Missions is God's invitation and His command to all of us is to be His hands and feet and His mouth in a hurting world. His call is to every follower to bear "fruit that will last."

Margaret Burks

I met Margaret Burks many years ago in Georgia. She was born in 1914 and became a CPA at age 39. She was a wife and an active church member. She did all the usual things women do in church, but she had a special love for missions organizations. She believed in teaching others about missions even though she never had the opportunity to go on a missions trip. One day after the death of her husband, the opportunity to go presented itself. At 70 years of age, Margaret went to Liberia to teach the Bible, swimming lessons, and crafts at a girls camp. That first experience changed her life. Over the next several years she went on numerous other missions trips to Liberia. Somehow she found herself, not at the girls camp, but on construction teams helping to build eight churches.

At age 75, with all her building experience behind her, Margaret decided to reroof the cafeteria at Camp Pinnacle, a Christian girls camp in Georgia. We were in need of so many things at the camp, and Margaret was determined to do all she could to help. I will never forget the day she challenged my teammates and me to a contest. Lockers, stacked in many pieces, needed to be put together so the girls could store their personal belongings when they came to camp the next summer. She looked me right in the eye and said: "My team can beat your team. We'll put more lockers together faster than your team can." With a faint hint of a smile the race was on. Several hours later, as you might expect, Margaret's team won! My team, all of us younger than Margaret by 30 years or more, ran out of time and energy!

After Margaret's 76th birthday, she decided she needed to know more about the Bible. She had taught the Bible for many years at her church, but sensing God's direction, she enrolled in a seminary in New Orleans, Louisiana. I remember the day her graduation invitation came. At age 81, Margaret graduated at the top of her class from New Orleans

Baptist Theological Seminary with a master of divinity degree in pastoral ministries. Her entire Sunday School class drove to New Orleans to be with her on that special day. You might think Margaret would have been willing to return home and enjoy the golden years of retirement. After all, she was 81 years old. Instead, four months later, Margaret went to Tanzania to teach Old Testament in the International Baptist Seminary. Her commitment to follow God's call had not ceased because of her age.

When Margaret went to Tanzania, once again God revealed how He uses every skill we have when needed to accomplish His purposes. With her skills as a CPA, she became the manager of the bookstore and treasurer of the church. As a result of all her years of teaching adults and children, she became the director of the women and children's division of the seminary. With her seminary training, she was able to disciple the future leaders of Tanzania and other countries represented at the seminary.

But Margaret's story doesn't end there. She came home after her 85th birthday, not because she wanted to or needed to, she quickly reminded me one day. And she hasn't stopped going to Africa just because she officially retired. She continues to make trips to Africa, offering her service to the work of the seminary and other individuals who are sharing the gospel. She is making a contribution for the future of missions in Georgia as well. One of the first things she did when she returned home was to organize ongoing missions education classes for all ages in her church. She is committed to passing on her passion for missions to the next generation and for following God's call.

When I attended Margaret's 90th birthday celebration in 2004, she was on her way "out West" to share her mission stories. It was obvious to me she is still on the journey of faith begun so many years ago. She is still living life to the fullest, making every day count. Her words and her actions match, and people notice. She is living the call with great joy and enthusiasm.

Giving our best

Babbs Douglas received professional training in music in college. She married a minister and found many ways to use her gifts in the church. She has a beautiful voice and is a frequent soloist in church performances, community choral presentations, and special civic events. As a wife and mother, she became engaged in activities through the school system and the community. She studied dance and found a place in the local dance company, performing regularly in such special events as the *Nutcracker*. She is a woman of many talents.

Professionally, Babbs has worked at a variety of jobs as opportunities presented themselves: in banking, as a secretary, but never in music. I always hoped that one day God would allow her to find a place of employment where her gifts would be used to the fullest. I was thinking about music, but God had other ideas. What a thrill it has been to watch Babbs develop into a businesswoman who is now the director of an area-wide food bank, part of the national Second Harvest Food Bank system. She spends her days loading and unloading 18-wheelers of food, supervising staff, operating a forklift when necessary, and developing and balancing budgets on a shoestring. She has a passion for feeding the hungry, especially children in the poverty areas of her city. She developed the program called Kids Café where hundreds of children are fed a hot meal once each day in their housing district. I have watched her grow the business to a capacity delivery program, providing food for the many ministries in her city that feed the hungry and the homeless. She is a frequent speaker at schools, churches, and civic groups, raising awareness of the needs of the hungry and the opportunities to eradicate hunger in her part of the world and beyond.

When you hear Babbs speak about the food bank, you realize immediately that God called her to serve in this role of a business executive. She sees her business as one of taking two loaves of bread and five small fishes and multiplying them for the masses like Jesus did. Music is still her first love, but only because it gives her a creative offering of thanks back to the Lord for His call in her life. For Babbs, her words of testimony are lived out each day as she serves the hungry in her hometown and as she models servant leadership to the business community.

Gert served for more than 20 years as a hospital nursing supervisor. She and her two young boys moved south to be near family after her husband, a New York police officer, was killed. She became active in a local church and a strong advocate for quality nursing practice in the hospital where she practiced. Working alongside her, I observed her passion for giving the best nursing care possible. She also loved and supported her nurses. On more than one occasion, I watched her speak out in our defense when we were challenged about our commitment to quality patient care, but she did it in the most loving way. I often said that when she addressed a controversial issue with someone, the other person was totally unaware they were being chastised at the time because she was so kind in the way she did it. I realized, as I discovered the depth of her faith, that was how she allowed Christ to be seen in her life and through her ministry as our leader.

Gert also believed that to be the best nurse possible, education was an ongoing commitment. When her sons went off to school, she went back to school and received her bachelor's degree; then decided to work towards her master's degree. I could not understand how she could work the long hours, do all that was required of her as our supervisor, and go to school at the same time. She was amazing. She was very focused and felt strongly that this was God's direction for her at this time in her life. It was obvious God had called her to the nursing profession and to her role as the leader of our nursing unit. In every way, with the patients, the staff, and visitors, she presented the gospel each day in her words and in her actions by the way she loved people.

When God calls us to follow Him, He uses whatever means we offer to make a difference in the lives of those we meet. He calls teachers to teach with all the gusto they can because of Him. He calls businessmen and -women to exercise their gifts with enthusiasm and integrity as they engage in the affairs of companies, government, and civic organizations. He calls nurses, doctors, pharmacists, and other medical personnel to represent Him in the kindest, most loving manner as they care for the sick and dying. We are called to allow the love of God to so permeate our lives that everything we do and all we become are a reflection of Christ.

Os Guinness says, "The motive, the initiative, and the action of calling are entirely God's and all of grace. Christ does not choose us because we are worth choosing, but simply because in his grace he loves us and chooses us—he calls us, in fact, despite all that he had to do to seal that choice in blood."[2]

Margaret, Babbs, and Gert's lives demonstrate the truth that God equips each of us with different sets of skills, abilities, and talents. His call confirms the truth that He has chosen us and gifted us uniquely for service. No one profession or role in the church, no one ministry or service, is better than another. When He calls us and we say yes, He empowers us to live the call to the fullest, giving God the best we have to offer. Paul told the Corinthians "whatever you do, do it all for the glory of God" (1 Corinthians 10:31).

Passing it on

How we live the call God places in our lives is often a direct reflection of many influences throughout our lives. Our early years with parents and experiences in school have a tremendous impact on who we become as adults. But they are not a license to accept a mediocre response to God's call. Good or bad, these experiences do not have the final say on who we are as adults. Christ is the ultimate and final influence, sifting through all of the things that make us who we are and bringing us to the person He wants us to be. He comes into our lives and draws together the best of all that is within us. He points us in the direction of a better way and places various influences and people in our paths to help shape our future.

Many of us have struggled with some aspects of our past experiences. Some people have allowed a negative past to prevent them from moving forward. But those who allowed their relationship with Christ to guide their future have emerged stronger. They have the opportunity to influence others who are beginning their journey of discovering God's call in a way that makes an eternal difference.

Looking back on my life, I realize I have been blessed with role models that I believe God placed in my life to help guide me through a critical time of decision making or significant life-changing experiences. As a freshman student at the school of nursing, I lived just down the hall from what we would call today the campus minister. Oma Dell Franklin (Ely now) was a gifted worker with students who listened to our stories or complaints, who provided opportunities for us to grow spiritually without forcing it on us, and who had a knack for knowing the exact moment we just needed a listening ear. Having lost my mother just before entering college, Oma Dell was a wise counselor for me during that first year. She seemed to see things in me that I did not see, the beginnings of leadership skills, a spiritual hunger that was seeking growth, and more. Because of her influence, I became involved in our local and state chapter of the Baptist Student Union, as it was called during those days, becoming the president during my senior year. This organization and many of the people I met had a tremendous impact on my life during those impressionable years as a college student. In her quiet, kind way Oma Dell influenced my life and understanding of my responsibility in missions in a positive way when I needed it most.

Live the Call

When I married my husband and went to our first church where Larry served as pastor, I knew very little about how to be the wife of a minister. I grew up in the church but had not ever really known a minister's wife personally. Three women in our church took a special interest in me, inviting me to their homes, to go on trips to state meetings, and to minister alongside them in community missions. They accepted me where I was in my spiritual journey and taught me about praying for missions and missionaries, about the Great Commission, and my responsibility to be a part of God's plan for reaching the world. They modeled for me what it meant to be a Christian wife, mother, and leader in the church. They even taught me how to cook many of the dishes I still prepare to this day for my family. Looking at my notebook of special recipes is like a walk back in time with many special memories attached. The names of Ara, Julia, and Snooks are all there and in so many other places in my home and in my heart.

Today we might call these role models *mentors*. Mentoring means a person invests themselves in the life of another person. They become a trusted guide, counselor, friend for someone who desires to mature in their faith, in their role as a parent, or in some ministry role. They become a significant influencer in the life of another person.

At the time, I had never heard the word *mentoring*, but I realize these women were doing just that for me. All I knew was that I felt love, acceptance, and encouragement to become the best I could be and to develop a heart for the world as God directed me. When we moved away from the church to the missions assignment overseas, looking back, I realize they continued to mentor me from a distance. When my name appeared for the first time on the missionary prayer calendar, it was a Sunday morning. The first call I received that morning was from Snooks who reminded me that at church that day they paused and prayed for me. Thousands of miles separated us, but through prayer they came alongside me in a special way, asking God to be present as I adjusted to my new home.

I believe I am the person I am today because I was blessed to have these early mentors, role models, in my life who helped shape my understanding of what it means to live the call of God.

Following Christ's example

Scripture, life experiences, and mentors all contribute to our understanding of how to live out the call God places in our lives. However, the greatest influence is the example of Jesus Himself. As followers of Christ we are called to serve others in the manner of Jesus. Scripture reminds us that He was always concerned about the needs of people and presented a model for us of how to meet those needs. He combined actions and words, ministry and witness, because He knew the importance of both; meeting a temporary need made it possible to offer an eternal gift, salvation. One day when Jesus was with the disciples, He was asked a question about when the end of the age would come. Always looking for the opportunity to teach them, Jesus responded with a story. A portion of that passage is a litany of words that reminds us how Jesus served others. It provides a word picture of who we are to serve, how we are to serve, and the spirit with which we are to serve today.

"Come, you who are blessed by my Father; take
your inheritance, the kingdom prepared for
you since the creation of the world.
For I was hungry and you gave me something to
eat,
I was thirsty and you gave me something to drink,
I was a stranger and you invited me in,
I needed clothes and you clothed me,
I was sick and you looked after me,
I was in prison and you came to visit me."
Then the righteous will answer him, "Lord, when
did we see you hungry and feed you, or thirsty
and give you something to drink? When did
we see you a stranger and invite you in, or
needing clothes and clothe you? When did we
see you sick or in prison and go to visit you?"
The King will reply, "I tell you the truth, whatever you did for one of the least of these
brothers of mine, you did for me."

Matthew 25:34–37

Jesus calls us to a life of service that is modeled after His
manner of service. We are called to be His disciples and
called to serve others in whatever way He leads us. Living
out His call in ministry and witness ensures that those who

are watching us day after day can trust our words because of the consistency they see in how we live. Living the call becomes a testimony to the power of God working in and through us. When we begin to understand that God is calling each of us, regardless of our professions, our family life, or our circumstances, to live the unique call He has for each one of us, our lives take on significance and meaning. We begin to find our way in how to "walk worthy," fully pleasing the Lord who loves us unconditionally and has chosen us to be one of His children.

Think about:

1. What does it mean to live the call?
2. How did God use the Habitat for Humanity project mentioned in this chapter to reach out to people in the community?
3. How has Margaret Burks lived the call?
4. What unique call have you experienced from God? How are you living the call?
5 What does mentoring mean? Who is a mentor to you?

CHAPTER 11

![chapter image]

PERSEVERE THROUGH DIFFICULTIES

"Who stands fast? Only the man whose final standard is not his reason, his principles, his conscience, his freedom, or his virtue, but who is ready to sacrifice all this when he is called to obedient and responsible action in faith and in exclusive allegiance to God—the responsible man, who tried to make his whole life an answer to the question and call of God."

Dietrich Bonhoeffer, from *Ethics*[1]

A few years ago I was invited to lead a retreat for American embassy, government, and business wives living in Nicaragua. Several missionary families were living in the country at the time and were invited to participate as well. Following the retreat, I visited with and observed those who had heard God's call to serve in this place, a war-torn part of the world that frequently made headlines in the news. Many of the women tried to explain why they were living in this country, and most said it was because of their husband's work. Many were counting the days until they could return to the US. All but one group—the missionaries. Missionaries are often the people who can most clearly put into words what it means to live the call God places in their lives. Maybe it is because of the struggle and challenge to leave the comfort of home and live cross-culturally; or maybe it is because they feel so deeply about the people they are called to serve. Whatever the reason, the missionaries in Nicaragua at that time helped me understand God's call in a significant way.

For a few days I stayed in the home of missionaries Keith and Penny Stamps and their two children. I observed how they worked through literature distribution to equip the national Christians to teach and share their faith with their own people. I helped Penny prepare for the women's craft class she taught, which served as a way for her to connect with other women and lead them in a Bible study.

One beautiful starry night I worshipped with a group of people I would never have imagined I would meet. A small group gathered in a three-sided shed to listen as Keith taught the Bible story through pictures. While I couldn't understand a word spoken, I understood the story because of the pictures; I knew the English words to the familiar hymns they were singing in Spanish. It was a great time of worship.

The more I learned about the people living on this hillside, the more I was reminded of God's ability to bring all people, even a divided people regardless of language or culture, to Him. Under the shed were Contras and Sandinistas, former guerrilla war enemies living, working, and now worshipping together on the same hillside; people who made a choice when the government offered them the option of giving up their weapons for a piece of land and a chance to begin life anew in peace. With this choice, they were discovering the truth of God's love because of the ministry of this missionary family.

As I watched Keith that night, I wondered where he gained the ability to relate so well to people whose lives were so foreign to anything most of us have ever experienced. As I learned more of their personal story, I was even more amazed at how God's call can be so compelling.

Keith and Penny Stamps grew up as missionaries' kids (MKs), living in South America. Their lives were far from the normal lifestyle of American kids. They grew up in a vastly different culture from most American teens. When it came time to go off to college, they faced a unique set of adjustments; they didn't just leave their family and home, they left their native country, culture, and language in addition to family.

Keith grew up in Ecuador. As God began to deal with him about his future, Keith shared one significant memory of a time when he knew God was calling him to a specific type of service. He and his family were spending a year back in the US and were attending a missions conference. Keith said, "As the week developed, I was moved in my heart, and after one morning's service walked forward under the intense conviction that God wanted me to serve in foreign missions. I had seen some men come to my father in Ecuador, asking him to send someone to their village to begin a church. I remembered his sorrow when there was no one to send."

Penny accepted Christ as her Savior as a child. Like most kids, she had her ups and downs in her walk with the Lord. By her second year of college, she began to sense that there was something more that God wanted of her. She and Keith had dated since high school, and she knew he had surrendered to the ministry. Penny said, "I came to realize that I needed to follow God's call in my life, whether it was with Keith or not. During my second year of college, I surrendered to full-time Christian service.

"Even though Keith and I knew that we were called to be missionaries by the time we were married, I realized that I needed to be willing to let go of some limits that I had placed on my willingness to go wherever God led. I had grown up in South America, but had always lived in a major city and attended North American schools. Now I had to be willing to consider living in a remote and rural area, where my children would not have other North American children to play with, and I would need to homeschool them. As I contemplated moving to an area that was guerrilla occupied, and where drug plants were grown, I had to learn to trust God with the safety of my family. Once I surrendered my own preconceived ideas and told God I would trust Him with my children, He gave a wonderful sense of peace and assurance that I was going where He wanted me to go."

This experience was to be repeated several times in the

years that followed. Living in a remote area of Guatemala during the years of civil war proved to be more difficult than Keith and Penny imagined. Penny became fearful for the well-being of her family. She realized she had to give her fear to God if she was going to be able to serve effectively. Penny remembers, "Early after moving to the village of Tajumulco and after several frightening experiences, I asked the Lord to take away my fear. I knew that I could not live in that place for long if I were going to always be afraid. God did take away my fear! And even though there were some dangerous moments, I was free from fear."

Some of the fear was based on incidents that would make any of us fearful and probably send most of us back to the US. At one point, the couple was accused of stealing children; someone rolled boulders down a hill onto their car; and they were temporarily displaced due to an injury her husband sustained. But the worst came two years later when Keith was shot in an attempted carjacking. Bleeding and seriously wounded, Keith managed to stay in control of the car and drive to a place for help. His recovery was long and difficult and required that their family return to the States. No one would have blamed them if they had remained in the US for good. After a time of healing and rehabilitation, they sensed God's call to return to missionary service. Rather than return to Guatemala, they accepted an assignment in Nicaragua.

Being in their home in Nicaragua and hearing some of their story helped me realize just how fitting it was for them to be working with these former fighters. In some way, because of their own experiences with violence, they could understand the kind of lives that these people had lived. They had experienced violence themselves, found their way through to forgiveness, and could now help the people that God called them to serve find their way to the love of a forgiving God.

Keith describes God's call this way: "God calls all His children to obedience. Our obedience requires us to adjust and grow and even sacrifice in all walks of life. No Christian is exempt. Obedience is necessary for a right relationship with Him. God rewards obedience. We must do what no one else is doing to reach those that no one else is reaching."

There have been other challenges as Keith and Penny followed God's call. Learning how to communicate with oral learners who cannot read Spanish, learning different dialects of the language groups they have worked with, not being able to be with family when death occurs or other times of personal family needs, and now not seeing their parents and children for long periods of time. Keith also reminds us "those involved in full-time Christian service are not exempt from the frustrations of daily life. Life overseas can multiply the frustrations as you face cross-cultural living and unexpected bureaucracy."

Keith and Penny have come full circle. They have followed God's call just as their parents did and have given their lives for reaching those who do not know Christ. They are watching and listening as their children each deal with God's specific call in their lives. Both have indicated God is calling them into some form of missions or full-time Christian service. What better resource for discerning God's call can these two young adults have than the example of grandparents and parents who have been on the same journey themselves throughout their lives.

Following God's call may not always be easy, but many people who have followed affirm that it is definitely worth it. Penny says in her own life: "Following God's call is an honor and privilege God gives to ordinary, weak people like me. Following His call brings peace and builds your faith and trust in Him. There is no greater joy than being in the center of God's will."

Today Keith and Penny are providing leadership for all of Mexico and Central America in the area of training leaders and developing storying tracks for chronological Bible storying as a means of sharing the gospel. They continue to live the call to missions that first came many years ago but is reaffirmed every day as they serve.

Continually listening

On this same trip to Nicaragua, I met another couple working in the same region, Jim and Viola Palmer. What has transpired in their lives since that visit is amazing. I thought both couples were doing significant work among people who had known nothing but war. I remember being amazed at the calmness they all exhibited with guards carrying rifles sitting around the clock outside the doors of their homes. I felt very uneasy as I ventured for the first time into a culture of unrest that is so prevalent. I had only caught a glimpse of this reality of life for so many people through the lens of the nightly news on American television. It was quite a different view in person. I also learned a new lesson about following God's call. His call is not always a one-time event to one particular place. Just like you and me, missionaries are called to continually listen, continually seek His way, and respond when He calls. It is a part of the challenge we all face as we live the call. For Jim and Viola, after years of serving as the leaders in Managua, God issued a new call

In a recent letter from Viola, a fellow nurse who is using her skills in far different ways than she once imagined, I learned just how difficult following God's call to a new place can be. When asked how she knew they were to make the move, she replied:

"For several years we had a request in to send a new missionary to the Mosquito Coast of Nicaragua and Honduras. My husband, Jim, was at a meeting with some of the leaders of the International Mission Board (IMB) when he asked why they had not been able to fill the request. The response was, 'Have you seen that request?' Jim replied, 'I wrote the request! I didn't want people to go there thinking it was an easy position. It will be difficult living in that environment and even more difficult ministering there.' The IMB representative asked if we had a veteran couple that would be willing to go, and Jim answered, 'Are you kidding? Have you seen that request?' After the laughter the IMB representative responded, 'If we don't have a veteran couple that already knows Spanish and would only have to learn Miskito language, and already knows church planting, and whose children are grown and wouldn't have to homeschool, what makes you think we can get a new couple that will have to learn two languages and how to church plant and homeschool their children?'

"Jim returned home and told me about the conversation and how discouraged he felt afterwards. Then he looked at me and asked, 'Do you think we could ever live out there?' I immediately responded, 'Yes! This is what God was preparing me for.' Jim and I decided to spend time praying about this possibility. As we began to feel this was the right direction, we shared with others our decision. We were affirmed in our decision by other Christians who told us they felt God was indeed calling us to serve with the Miskito people."

When Jim and Viola first arrived on the coast six years ago, there were 7 small congregations. Today, they have seen God plant more than 100 churches. Christians have taken on more and more responsibility for the work, and they have seen God answer prayer instantly. Viola said: "We have seen miracles in people's lives." But even with complete assurance that God was calling them, the work has not been easy. When asked about living in this remote region, Viola shared that the "work is physically challenging, emotionally trying, and the only way to stay sane is to seek God each day. It is more difficult to not have adequate health care. There is no infrastructure in this area of Nicaragua or Honduras. There have been times when roads were not passable or bridges were out or rivers were too flooded or too dry to safely maneuver. We have had to spend nights in areas that were not safe, much less comfortable. I would say the challenge is to stay consistently in contact with God each and every day; to trust God with the large and small things of life."

Despite all the difficulties, Viola believes they are following God's call and it has been worth it. "When you follow God's will, He will bless you and show you His face through the lives of His people. Your life will be full and rich. It will NOT be boring!"

Obeying

God's call in our lives is a very personal experience. In the daily discovery of who God is and how He wants to guide us in living, we also discover He wants to guide what we do. We make our own plans every day, but the truth is, His plans are always the best. Since the choice is always ours, the question becomes: Are we willing to settle for less than His best?

In a recent sermon, my pastor talked about the path of developing character traits as a follower of Christ. He said each of us face choices each day. Before we come to faith, we basically focus on choosing between right and wrong. But once we become followers of Christ, the choice should no longer be between right and wrong. It should be about choosing what is good, better, or best in any given situation; between what is the right thing to do, what will lead us to serve others, and what becomes sacrifice on our part for the sake of God's kingdom. If we focus on things that are less than God's best for our lives, we can never attain the character traits of Christ, much less experience His best gifts for our lives.

God's call is a journey that moves us along a path of learning to do what is right in everyday situations to living a life of service that makes a difference in the lives of others. Eventually, that path leads us to discover what sacrificial living means as we follow Christ into the world.

Scripture verifies that God's call is often a test of obedience. In the Book of Genesis, in the midst of God's unhappiness and sorrow over the state of His creation, God saw one man who was good—Noah. He planned to destroy all that He created, but He gave Noah a choice. He called him to follow what must have seemed like the craziest of plans—

build a boat in the desert. It was a call to obedience, to follow God's instructions exactly as He laid them out. Because Noah trusted God, he answered the call and obeyed. Genesis 7:5 says, "And Noah did all that the Lord commanded him."

Noah and his entire family were saved and became God's instruments for starting over with His highest creation. Because of Noah, God once again saw the beauty of His creation, giving the rainbow as a sign of His promise, a covenant, to never destroy life again. God said: "I now establish my covenant with you and with your descendants after you and with every living creature that was with you. . . . I have set my rainbow in the clouds" (Genesis 9:9–10, 13). Noah was obedient when God called.

Following God's call to a new way of life or a new place of service is always a challenge. But when you have served Him faithfully in what you already thought was the hard place, and He asks us to move to a place even more difficult might be hard for any of us. I like the words on the sign that hangs in the ministry center where Jim and Viola Palmer work, "If you want to hear God laugh, tell Him your long-range plans."

Living the call

At the 1992 WMU Annual Meeting in Indianapolis, Rebecca Carnell, a professional banker, saw a video about teaching people to read. The gentleman in the video stated that his learning to read was a miracle and expressed his gratitude for the woman who taught him. In that instant, Rebecca heard God's call to literacy missions. Having been previously trained in a literacy workshop, she became convicted about putting her knowledge into practice. She sought advanced training and began to train others in teaching adult reading and writing as well as conversational English to internationals.

In 1998, after six years of volunteering, she and her husband realized God was calling her to leave her banking career and work full time in literacy missions. With her family's blessing, Rebecca began to devote all her time to this ministry. Shortly after making this commitment, Rebecca faced a serious challenge, one that could have destroyed not only her ministry, but also her entire life. Rebecca's husband, a truck driver, was involved in a serious accident in another state. Two people were killed, and he was blamed for the accident; he has been in prison in another state ever since. This single event could have destroyed their lives, but God took the worst of circumstances and turned them into good. Rebecca's literacy work has flourished, and her husband is now involved in ministry within the walls of the prison where he lives.

Today Rebecca provides leadership to her state by helping them see the need and seize opportunities to reach people for Christ through literacy missions. The world has literally come to our doorstep, and Rebecca realizes we have an incredible opportunity to reach the world by connecting with those who come to our country if only for a brief time. A side effect of this has been how others have watched and been affected by Rebecca's experience. People watch her to see how she will handle this adversity in her own life. How does she allow it to affect her commitment to the Lord and to following His call to missions? Her faithfulness has been a testimony of the steadfast love of God for His children and has made a lasting impact on the lives of so many people for the cause of Christ. Rebecca Carnell is living proof of the power of God at work in our lives and what it means to live the call every day.

Making a choice

It is often said that one of the hardest places in the entire world to live faithfully as a follower of Christ is in the home. Those who live with us each and every day see us at our best and also at our worst. The challenge becomes even greater when a spouse or children are not believers. We bear a great responsibility as we witness with our words and actions. How we handle the day-to-day stresses of life validates or invalidates the power of Christ to work in our lives. None of us are perfect, and aren't we glad that Christ does not demand perfection? But perhaps the greatest testimony we offer in the home is how we handle our moments of imperfection. Mistakes and failure are a part of all our lives. Admitting our failures, asking for forgiveness from God and the family member we offended, can be a most powerful tool in sharing how the Christian life works. Helping one another to see the Christian faith as a journey of becoming frees up everyone in the family to be real, to be open and trusting of one another.

One of the greatest joys in my life is the privilege of being a wife, mother, and now a new grandmother. It is also the place where I have learned the most about what it means to be a follower of Christ. My children, especially, have taught me about persevering through hard days, about never giving up on a dream, about being willing to risk the known for the unknown. As all mothers have experienced, the children have, at times, tested my faith in God and my patience, but even in those moments, we all were learning how to follow Christ better. Over the past years as I have stretched to become a stronger leader for WMU, my children have been, next to my husband, my greatest source of encouragement.

When our daughter, Allison, was born, she was the first preacher's baby born into the church in almost 20 years. She was loved, pampered, and affirmed from the first day of her life. She was a true church baby, always being there whenever the doors of the church were open, and she loved it! By the age of two she was making pastoral calls with her daddy and always came home with a little reminder of the visit. Well, all but one. The day an elderly member gave her a chicken as a pet my husband very wisely asked if the chicken could continue to live at her house, not ours.

Allison was five when we heard God's call to mission service. We worried about how we would tell her and how she would react to our moving away from the only home she had ever known. The day came when we knew we had to begin preparing her for what was ahead. We began by describing the beautiful island with water all around, the beaches, and the bananas growing on every tree when she suddenly stopped us and with great excitement asked if we were moving to Upper Volta. She was ready to go as a missionary because her Mission Friends® teacher, Miss Ruth, taught her all about being an MK in Africa. She never looked back from that day on until we arrived in St. Vincent, teaching me how to anticipate with joy the future God was preparing.

Allison has carried that commitment to serve others for the cause of Christ with her to this very day. I've watched her struggle to discern God's call in her life in college when her love for music and piano came into conflict with her desire to improve the lives of women and children caught in the cycle of abuse. When she ultimately decided to go to law school so she could advocate for better laws and defend the rights of women, it was a struggle. Her artistic side fought the rigid, legalistic thinking required, but she never gave up. I think the thing I respect and admire most in her is that no matter how hard it was, no matter how discouraged she became, she never lost sight of the fact God had called her, and He would see her through. Even today when the caseload is heavy, when her heart breaks over a client caught up in domestic violence, she presses on because of His call.

Matthew was born three and one-half years after his sister. We often comment that Allison is a lot like her father—creative, artsy, good with words. Matt is like me with his love for science, math, and medicine. Like his mother, he is also a sucker for any child selling cookies or candy that comes to our door.

When he was five and we were living back in the US, he made a puzzle in Mission Friends one night and hurried to show it to his dad. On the way to Larry's office, a piece of the puzzle fell off without his knowing it. When he made it to Larry's desk and put the puzzle down, he became quite upset. He had spelled out the word *missions*, but one letter was missing. "I've lost the *I* out of missions!" he exclaimed. In his young mind, missions was a part of what all followers of Christ were to be a part of and the most important part was missing when the *I* was lost.

Missions has always been a part of Matt's life. Through the years, He has consistently been the one in his class at school or church to initiate missions projects, always looking for ways to help someone less fortunate. As he moved through high school and into college, he began to sense God calling him to some kind of profession in medicine. He had watched me use my nursing skills in various ways and his father serve as a hospital chaplain. He always said one day he wanted to go with me on a medical missions trip. I'll never forget our first time of serving side by side through medical clinics in Bosnia in 1999. When we finished our work for the day, the adults feeling exhausted, I watched Matt seek out neighborhood children and teach them to play baseball or play with a soccer ball. He was always the first one to encourage the team to get into the culture, to try some new food or meet new people. He was the one willing to go the extra mile for someone in need of medicine, making pharmacy runs frequently. Matt reminded me on this trip how to be curious about new cultures and to laugh at the unexpected.

As an asthmatic child, Matt faced many obstacles from a physical aspect. He always found a way to participate in sports in whatever way he could and discovered a love for singing that gave him a unique focus. By his example, he taught me how to work around whatever roadblocks were placed in our paths. He has affirmed the truth that if God is calling you to something, He will make it possible. Today Matt is completing the next step in his own professional and spiritual journey as he completes graduate school to become a physician's assistant and continues his call to serve others. Wherever that call takes him, I am confident God's call will be what guides his decisions.

Live the Call

There are many times when God will call us to a task or a place that will be difficult. We can meet the challenge head-on or walk away; it's our choice. But by heeding Paul's admonition to "walk worthy" we can find the strength and the courage to live the call and reap the blessing that comes from following Christ.

Dietrich Bonhoeffer asked, "Who stands fast?" The answer rings true: the one "who is ready to sacrifice all this when he is called to obedient and responsible action in faith and in exclusive allegiance to God—the responsible man, who tried to make his whole life an answer to the question and call of God."

Think about:

1. What are some of the roadblocks that Keith and Penny Stamps face in their ministry?
2. How do they eliminate these roadblocks?
3. How did Jim and Viola Palmer answer a special call in Nicaragua?
4. Where is one of the hardest places to live faithfully as a follower of Christ?
5. What are some of the roadblocks you find to living faithfully at home?

CHAPTER 12

THE ULTIMATE REWARD

"Answering the call of our Creator is 'the ultimate why' for living, the highest source of purpose in human existence. Apart from such a calling, all hope of discovering purpose will end in disappointment."

Os Guinness, *The Call*[1]

Sitting on the cold concrete floor of the customs storage room, I began to wonder if I had heard God's call correctly. As we counted every pill in every bottle of medicine and listed it on legal page after legal page, I wondered if we would ever be allowed to serve the refugees of the Balkan War as we planned. Under the watchful eye of customs officials, we were careful not to make mistakes, to toss any out-of-date medicines, and to smile at the guard regardless of what was being said. We tried to make the best of a somewhat uncertain situation. Several hours later, with every box counted and documented, we left wondering if we would ever see any of the thousands of dollars of donated medicines and supplies again.

Once back at the volunteer house we met as a team to discuss plan B should we have only our skills as nurses and what little medicine we could pool together from our luggage with which to operate the clinics. Our call had been to meet the physical needs of refugees pouring into Sarajevo, Bosnia, from places throughout the Balkans where war was still raging. Medical clinics, we hoped, would open the doors for our Baptist partners living in the country to share Christ with so many who did not know Him. Discouraged, wondering if we could follow through with our commitment to serve, we began to pray. God reminded us that He alone would bring to pass His desire regardless of our plans or the perceived obstacles. His call was simply to follow Him in faith and obedience.

Over the next few days while we waited for a decision from customs, we responded to several requests to meet refugees and evaluate their medical needs. A small group had found refuge in a school while students were away on a school break. They told us about a mother who had a handicapped child that was hospitalized. Everyone seemed very concerned and wished she could meet with us. We promised to return on another day.

Late the next evening we received word the mother had returned to the school and asked to meet with the American nurses. Through our interpreter, we heard her story of leaving in the night with only limited clothes and medicine when the war came to her village. Her child had a form of epilepsy and took a special German-made drug. She only had a few doses left, and the hospital had nothing to give her. She was not Bosnian. She did not have proper credentials to receive medical care and medicines even if they had the drug. Trying to soothe her worried spirit I promised we would do all we could to find the medication. I did not realize at the time just what I had promised.

The next day, customs released our supplies and the medical clinics began, always moving to a new location each day. As nurses we were able to help many who came and our translators made sure the people knew we were followers of Christ there to serve ALL nationalities. In the midst of busy, long days, the needs of the mother and her child with epilepsy were never far from my mind. In each area where we held a clinic I would visit the local pharmacy to ask about the drug. Always the same answer—it's a German drug and will not be found in Bosnia. Sometimes in the midst of so many with great needs we have a tendency to zero in on one need and strive with all our might to meet the one need. That was the case for me. With each passing day as our time in the country grew shorter and shorter, I became more and more focused on finding this one medication. In great frustration one day, I cried out to the Lord, "Please help me meet this one need, and I'll know why you brought me to this place." The final day arrived and still no medicine.

After lunch, while the team was packing up remaining supplies and preparing to return home, I asked my interpreter if we could try a few more small, out-of-the-way pharmacies. He agreed to drive me, and as had been the case each day, with no results. On our way back to the volunteer house, after stopping at a grocery store, I looked across the highway and saw a small pharmacy under an apartment-housing complex. Looking at my interpreter I begged for one more stop. By this time he knew of my deep desire to meet this one need, and he agreed but with little hope of finding the drug.

Once again I told my story, showed the pharmacist the name of the drug, and waited for the usual negative response. But this time the pharmacist, who spoke English, had a very puzzled look on her face. After a moment she pulled two boxes of the very drug I was looking for out from under the counter and said, "I have been wondering why this drug was here and what I would do with it since it is not a legal drug in Bosnia." My heart did a flip, and I could hardly speak. We paid for the medication, and I knew God was performing a miracle. The next challenge was just as great, finding the mother who was forced to move from the school when the students returned. We only had a few hours of daylight left, and I had no idea where she lived. The school simply said someone gave her a room in an apartment once the child was released from the hospital. As we pulled out of the parking lot wondering which direction to go first, I noticed a veiled woman coming out of a neighborhood store with a loaf of bread. I knew in my heart it was the mother regardless of what my interpreter thought. I jumped out of the car, called her by name, and when the woman turned around it was the mother. I held up the boxes of medicine and ran to her. With tears in her eyes she embraced me and said the only English word I understood—*sister*. Over and over she hugged me and said, "Sister." I knew God had given me a great gift, an answer to my prayer to meet this one specific need. God didn't have to do it, but I believe He wanted to do a work in her life, to tell her of a God who meets the needs of an unbelieving Muslim mother. I also believe He wanted to work in my life affirming His call placed long before—a call to service in His name. It was a reminder of His faithfulness to hear and answer the prayers of His children.

The next day, we boarded the plane for home. Like many on the team, I spent a good bit of time reflecting on all we saw and experienced. The schedule of clinics, the kind of work, the witness given, had not quite matched our original plan, but I knew it was in God's plans, His design for our lives at this particular time in a faraway land. God's call is not always easy. It is not always revealed as an answer to a specific prayer. But God's call is always the best way, the best direction for our lives. To live the call and witness the miracles only God can provide is the most rewarding experience in life. On a final day of a long two weeks of seeking to be faithful to God's call, He spoke in a miraculous way, affirming for me that living the call truly makes life worthwhile.

There is much talk today about living successfully versus living a life of significance. Each of us, no matter life's circumstances, at some level have a desire to know without a doubt that when our life on earth is over, someone will know we have lived. That something we said or did made a difference in this world or at least in the life of another person.

Jesus came to make a difference, not only in the world at large, but personally in our lives as well. He came to show us a better way. With only two words, "Follow me," Jesus changed the lives of the disciples and history forever. He is still calling people today with those same two words. His is a call to a life of faith, commitment, and service. It begins when we come to Him acknowledging our sins and accepting God's wonderful gift of love and forgiveness. As we enter into a life lived in relationship to Christ, we are called to follow Him into the world, demonstrating His love through our words and actions. He invites us to discover that unique plan He has for our lives and allow Him to guide us as we follow.

Living out God's call is one of the most exciting and challenging experiences any follower of Christ can discover. It leads us into an ever-deepening awareness of the depth of God's love for us as His children. The apostle Paul reminds us of the depth of God's love in this passage from Romans:

"Who shall separate us from the love of Christ? Shall trouble or hardship or persecution or famine or nakedness or danger or sword? . . . No, in all these things we are more than conquerors through him who loved us. For I am convinced that neither death nor life, neither angels nor demons, neither the present nor the future, nor any powers, neither height nor depth, nor anything else in all creation, will be able to separate us from the love of God that is in Christ Jesus our Lord."

Romans 8:35, 37–39

In understanding just how much God loves us, we discover His promises to be with us forever, to sustain us through difficult days, and to celebrate with us when we find joy, are true. His call will be heard in many different ways: through the prayer of a friend; a still, small voice heard during your quiet time; or simply through the growing awareness as you read and study His Word. However, when a person hears God's call, the real challenge is to live the call with conviction and a strong commitment to be the presence of Christ in our world.

Several years after my trip to Bosnia, I went back to visit more of the countries that make up the Balkans. On that trip, I met a man of extraordinary courage and leadership who had heard God's call and stepped out with great faith. As a believer for many years, he served as a pastor of a small Baptist congregation in the beautiful mountains of Croatia. He is a humble man with great love for not only his own people but for all of God's people.

When war broke out in Bosnia, it wasn't long before it spilled over into neighboring countries, including Croatia. Refugees from many areas in the region fled their homes in the middle of the night with nothing but the clothes on their back. Stevo led his small church to begin assisting the refugees with food, clothing, and places to sleep. It was difficult for the church. They were few in number and had few resources, but Stevo led them in creative approaches to ministries. He saw the pain and suffering of the refugees because of the abuses inflicted during the war. During the time they ministered, he began to feel God was calling his church into a much different role than before the war, one of reconciliation and healing for people of all different backgrounds.

As I listened to Stevo's story, the significance of his decision to follow God's new call in his life dawned on me. He and his people were Croats—followers of Jesus Christ. There had been much killing and torture of all kinds inflicted on the Croats by Bosnian Muslims and Serbs in addition to revenge killings on the part of his own people. He had every right to refuse to minister to those who were not Croats. Religious intolerance had led to the most severe bloodshed in his country that he had ever known. He could have followed the path of many in his country, seeking revenge, but he heard God's voice calling him to share the love of Christ and His message of salvation, specifically with the Bosnian people.

After the war, borders of all the newly aligned countries were drawn. Many refugees returned home or sought asylum in other countries. What once was one country, Yugoslavia, where Serbs, Croats, and Bosnians lived together in relative peace, was now a land divided into many countries. Border crossings were lined with soldiers to keep the people separated. No one could cross over without special permission, and even that was difficult to obtain. How could Stevo respond to God's call in his life in a way that would bring the one true message of peace to hurting people? With all the restrictions on travel he knew he could not physically go to Bosnia. And then he knew—the Bosnians did not have the Bible in their own language. The Bible could speak where Stevo could not go. He began to work full time securing translators and all the legal permissions to translate the Bible. It took him four years, a lot of hard work, and his own personal savings plus the investment of others who caught a vision of Stevo's call from God.

What a special privilege it was to be sitting at the lunch table with Stevo when he received word that the newly translated Bible had reached Bosnia. With the help of other believers who were allowed to live in the country, this translation of the Bible had already been placed in thousands of homes. I watched this humble servant weep with joy over hearing the news that God's Word was being received by people that so many in his country hated.

I realized the cost, sacrifice, and personal commitment it must have taken for this miracle to take place. Stevo is a man who wanted to give something of significance back to God because of the deep gratitude he felt for God's blessings in his own life. He is an example to his people today—a man who overcame hatred and grief for the sake of the pure joy of living God's call. As a result, he is making a lasting difference in the lives of all who will read this Bible.

Following His will

There are people all around us who are discovering the peace and joy of living the call of God. One of those is a friend named Joy who has answered God's call in many different ways in her life. Joy says, "The most significant call came when Christ called me to Him as an older teenager, and I became a believer. I had not grown up in a church, and therefore, knew very little about the Bible or church. A couple of years later, as I had grown in understanding my relationship to Christ but was still new in my faith, I felt a distinct calling to a church-related vocation. However, I was ignorant of what opportunities were even possible, so I simply committed my life to do His will wherever it might lead.

"Following His will through a number of years and various circumstances led me to understand the global dimension of discipleship. Ultimately, that grew to a level of understanding God's 'sentness,' and I responded positively to be sent as a missionary in Japan. However, I've never placed specific geographical boundaries on that missions calling."

God's call did include a time of serving in Japan, and in many ways this period of service prepared her for an even more challenging role—to become the state executive director for WMU of Texas. Joy's experiences in Japan brought a depth of understanding in her missions commitment that only comes with personal experience. As a mentor to students and those she worked with in Japan, Joy brought those same skills into the WMU leadership network and helped other new leaders find their place in effective service. Her willingness to give of herself and the resources of her state to those in need endeared her to many young leaders. Her pure delight in serving the Lord is so evident to all who know her. When asked what it means to live the call she responded simply by saying, "Being obedient to God's call on my life means a joy that has nothing to do with outward circumstances but everything to do with an inward condition."

That inward condition is the transformation that takes place when Christ is the Lord of our lives. Living God's call moves us from seeking to be successful to living a life that makes a difference—a life of worth, value, and significance.

Sharing Jesus' cross

Early in my time of service at WMU, I met a wonderful woman who serves in a similar role as executive director of Korea WMU. Sook Jae Lee and I have many things in common. We are both nurses, love WMU and the avenue of service it provides, and we both have experienced God's call to move outside the place we thought would mark our lives. As I have visited with her in this country and recently in her own office, I have learned more about this incredible woman who leads Asian women to discover God's call for their lives. Here is her story:

"I received Jesus Christ as my Savior and Lord at age 16 during Girls in Action® (GA®) camp. After I received Jesus, God called me to serve Him as a nurse and a missionary. I became a registered nurse and served at the Wallace Memorial Baptist Hospital in Pusan, taught at the nursing college, and served rural people as a nurse practitioner and midwife for about 17 years. During that time, I considered myself a home missionary.

In 1979, God gave me a chance to attend the international community health seminar-workshop in Sri Lanka for three weeks. I could see the people there were poor, not only physically but also spiritually. I was very much challenged at that time to be a medical missionary to South East Asia. I served in a rural area as a community health nurse practitioner for about 3 years in preparation to be a missionary. It was a great joy for me to see a church started and more and more people become Christians before I left there. God answered my prayers.

"While I was working in a rural area, I was invited to be the future executive director of Korea national Baptist WMU (KBWMU). First, I refused because I believed that I was called as a medical missionary. After praying for 2 years, I knew that God wanted me to accept this position, and I surrendered to His call. I realized working with WMU is also being a missionary!"

I asked Sook Jae what it means to her today to follow God's call in the role of a leader of WMU instead of a nurse. She said it means she is "to share Jesus' cross; it is a meaningful and satisfying life. I have joy and peace in my heart. Every day I am excited and anticipate the great things will He do through me and KBWMU. He shows me that He is my Lord every day. I believe God has a plan for everyone. If He calls us, we have to obey God's will, because it is the best way for our life to glorify Him."

Indeed Sook Jae's life glorifies the Lord she serves. The outreach of Korea WMU within their own country and beyond is a testimony of the vision God has given this incredible leader. She has discovered as Guinness reminds us in his book, *The Call*, "Answering the call of our Creator is 'the ultimate why' for living, the highest source of purpose in human existence. Apart from such a calling, all hope of discovering purpose will end in disappointment. To be sure, calling is not what it is commonly thought to be. It has to be dug out from under the rubble of ignorance and confusion.

And, uncomfortably, it often flies directly in the face of our human inclinations. But nothing short of God's call can ground and fulfill the truest human desire for purpose."² *What is the result of following God's call?* The most frequent response to the question is always tied to the feeling of joy and peace that comes from God. But it is more than a feeling. It is an ever-growing awareness deep within our soul that God is truly fulfilling that deepest hunger to know why we are here and what makes life really worthwhile. Living the call is the only way to discover the best God has to offer for our lives.

Think about:

1. How did God use a pharmacist and a small pharmacy under an apartment-housing complex in Bosnia during the missions trip mentioned in this chapter? What would have happened if Wanda Lee had allowed the roadblock to keep her from going to this pharmacy?

2. What roadblocks did Stevo have to move to be able to reach out to refugees of the Bosnian war?

3. Why was Sook Jae's decision to lead Korea WMU so difficult?

4. What is "the ultimate why" for living, the reason we are here?

5. What can you do right now to increase your commitment to live the call?

LIVE THE CALL

Calling is one of the great mysteries of the Christian life. For the man or woman living outside of a personal relationship with Christ, calling will always remain hidden. But for those who have begun the journey by saying yes to Christ's invitation to "come, follow me," calling becomes the pathway to a life filled with incredible joy and peace. It is not a pathway free of roadblocks or challenges or questions. As a matter of fact, God's call often creates the bumps in our known and comfortable path.

God calls us to love Him with all we have—our heart, soul, mind, and strength. Loving Him frees us to receive a depth of love that no one else or no other thing can deliver. His love frees us to love others in a way that brings healing and joy to their lives and it frees us to love ourselves just as we are—weak, fallible, and far from perfect. His love makes us believe we can live His call because we can trust Him to provide all we will need.

I have heard God's call in the quiet corners of my mind and heart at various times in my life. Those times were so profound and so clearly heard that my life direction changed each time. You may be wondering if you have ever heard God's call. Think about the times in your life when you have been faced with major decisions. If you went seeking God's direction, what happened? What did it feel like once you made the choice? Did you have a sense of peace and joy that just overwhelmed you? A sense of *this is so right*, and you knew God had answered? Os Guinness said it so well, "Calling is the truth that God calls us to himself so decisively that everything we are, everything we do, and everything we have is invested with a special devotion and dynamism lived out as a response to his summons and service."[1]

It is never too late to understand God is calling you to embrace His design for your life. The best He has to offer, not just success in our lives, but significance, is yours for the asking. His call draws us to His design for our lives with incredible power. To live the call is to discover the answer to the ultimate questions we all ponder at some point in our lives: Why am I here, and what makes life worth it?

NOTES

Chapter 1
[1]David Brainerd quote, ChristianQuotes.org, http://www.christian quotes.org/results.php (accessed February 8, 2006).
[2]Os Guinness, *The Call: Finding and Fulfilling the Central Purpose of Your Life* (Nashville: W Publishing Group, 1998), 1.
[3]John Tadlock, *When It's Rush Hour All Day Long* (Birmingham, AL: New Hope Publishers, 2003), 24.
[4]Guinness, *The Call*, 4.

Chapter 2
[1]Os Guinness, *The Call: Finding and Fulfilling the Central Purpose of Your Life* (Nashville: W Publishing Group, 1998), 66.

Chapter 3
[1]Fisher Humphreys, *I Have Called You Friends* (Birmingham, AL: New Hope Publishers, 2005), 36.
[2]Minette Drumwright, *The Life That Prays* (Birmingham, AL: Woman's Missionary Union, 2001), 41–42.
[3]Stuart Calvert, *Uniquely Gifted* (Birmingham, AL: New Hope Publishers, 1993), 10.
[4]Barbara Joiner, *Yours for the Giving*, rev ed. (Birmingham, AL: New Hope Publishers, 1999), 77.
[5]Calvert, *Uniquely Gifted*, 13.

Chapter 4
[1]Michael Foust, "Barna: Biblical Worldview Held by Only 4% of Adults," *BP News* (Nashville: Baptist Press, December 2, 2003).

Chapter 5
[1]Janet Hoffman, *God Is Calling You* (Birmingham, AL: New Hope Publishers, 2002), 39.
[2]Ibid., 112–13.

[3]R. Daniel Watkins, *Encyclopedia of Compelling Quotations* (Peabody, MA: Hendrickson Publishers, Inc., 2002), 92.
[4]Ibid., 238.
[5]Ibid., 111.

Chapter 6
[1]Os Guinness, *The Call: Finding and Fulfilling the Central Purpose of Your Life* (Nashville: W Publishing Group, 1998), 46.
[2]Jim Cymbala, *Fresh Wind, Fresh Fire* (Grand Rapids, MI: Zondervan Publishing House, 1997).
[3]R. Daniel Watkins, *Encyclopedia of Compelling Quotations* (Peabody, MA: Hendrickson Publishers, Inc., 2002), 175.
[4]Calvin Partain, *Trusted Steward* (Birmingham, AL: Woman's Missionary Union, 1996), 3–6.
[5]Ibid., 6.
[6]Guinness, *The Call*, 46.

Chapter 7
[1]R. Daniel Watkins, *Encyclopedia of Compelling Quotations* (Peabody, MA: Hendrickson Publishers, Inc., 2002), 172.
[2]Ibid., 302.

Chapter 8
[1]Sherwood Wirt and Kersten Beckstrom, *Topical Encyclopedia of Living Quotations* (Minneapolis, MN: Bethany House, 1982), 75.
[2]Timothy George, *Faithful Witness: The Life and Mission of William Carey* (Birmingham, AL: New Hope Publishers, 1991), 32.
[3]Ibid.
[4]Dellanna O'Brien, *Timeless Virtues* (Birmingham, AL: New Hope Publishers, 2002), 189–90.
[5]Ibid., 191.

Chapter 9
[1]William Barclay, *The Letters to the Philippians, Colossians, and Thessalonians* (Philadelphia: Westminster Press, 1954, 1957, 1959), 126–27.
[2]Malcolm O. Tolbert, *Layman's Bible Book Commentary*, (Nashville: Broadman Press, 1980), 22:42.

[3]Harold S. Songer, *Colossians: Christ Above All* (Nashville: Convention Press, 1973), 25.
[4]Os Guinness, *The Call: Finding and Fulfilling the Central Purpose of Your Life* (Nashville: W Publishing Group, 1998), 206.

Chapter 10
[1]R. Daniel Watkins, *Encyclopedia of Compelling Quotations* (Peabody, MA: Hendrickson Publishers, Inc., 2002), 654.
[2]Os Guinness, *The Call: Finding and Fulfilling the Central Purpose of Your Life* (Nashville: W Publishing Group, 1998), 209.

Chapter 11
[1]Os Guinness, *The Call: Finding and Fulfilling the Central Purpose of Your Life* (Nashville: W Publishing Group, 1998), 94.

Chapter 12
[1]Os Guinness, *The Call: Finding and Fulfilling the Central Purpose of Your Life* (Nashville: W Publishing Group, 1998), 4.
[2]Ibid.

Live the Call
[1]Os Guinness, *The Call: Finding and Fulfilling the Central Purpose of Your Life* (Nashville: W Publishing Group, 1998), 4.

New Hope® Publishers is a division of WMU®, an international organization that challenges Christian believers to understand and be radically involved in God's mission. For more information about WMU, go to www.wmu.com. More information about New Hope books may be found at www.newhopepublishers.com. New Hope books may be purchased at your local bookstore.